PAY ATTENTION, SAY THANK YOU

SEVEN RULES & PRACTICES
FOR JOYFUL LIVING

M. GAIL WOODARD

MJF BOOKS

NEW YORK

Published by MJF Books
Fine Communications
322 Eighth Avenue
New York, NY 10001

Pay Attention, Say Thank You
LC Control Number: 2015951406
ISBN 978-1-60671-333-4

Note:
The ideas, suggestions and practices offered in this book are generic in
nature and have been gathered from a wide variety of sources. Neither the
author nor the publisher is engaged in providing medical or psychological
advice. In dealing with any medical or mental health condition, always
consult a physician or mental health professional.

This edition is published by MJF Books in arrangement
with Dudley Court Press.

Designed by Lisa Chovnick

Printed in the United States of America.

MJF Books and the MJF colophon are trademarks of Fine Creative Media, Inc.

QF   10   9   8   7   6   5   4   3   2   1

DEDICATION

To my Reader Group, who valiantly slogged through the early versions, chapter by chapter, reaching out with comments that lifted the quality of my thinking through each succeeding draft, and especially to those who called or emailed at just the right moment to lift me from the fen

— thank you.

To every single person whose life has touched mine, yielding the experiences and movement that have brought me to where I am now

— thank you.

To my three sons, Duncan, Reed and Casey, who graciously accept their mother's eccentricities and are willing to share her words and projects with their friends

— thank you.

To Bob, who allows, receives and loves all that I am

— thank you.

CONTENTS

Contents

PREFACE

In June 2005, on my way home to California after an eight-day yoga retreat in Greece, I spent two days in Paris. One of my goals was to visit the Rodin Museum, which I had not managed to see on three previous visits to Paris.

On Sunday morning, I took the subway to Varenne station and walked the short distance to 79 rue de Varenne, address of the Musée Rodin. The main entrance was under construction, so I continued a half block down the street to the temporary gate. After I paid my admission fee, I wandered into the grand estate, eyes on my visitors' map, deciding which to enjoy first, the main house or the vast garden.

I became aware of some statues to my left and realized that Rodin's huge masterpiece, *The Gates of Hell*, was right there against the hedges. I purposely turned away and walked forty or fifty feet down the path to the right so that my first impression of the sculpture would be from a proper angle.

When I was about fifty feet from the sculpture, I turned to take it in.

As if blasted by a hurricane wind, my body was thrust backward, pushed away by the pain and suffering still silently screaming from the 180 chilling figures caught in the bronzed portals of hell. I reacted with an audible "No! No more suffering!"

Breathing hard, and barely aware that I was talking aloud—to the sculpture, to Rodin, to God, to I don't know whom—I looked again at the twenty-foot-tall sculpture and heard myself declare again, "No more suffering. We have to live *love* now. We *can* live in love now!"

Backing away from the sculpture, I settled down. My intense reaction baffled me. Although I was in a heightened state of awareness after the yoga retreat, I had no preconceived notions, nor much specific knowledge about Rodin, his sculptures, his life or anything else that would have served as a catalyst for such a response to *The Gates of Hell*. All I knew was that I felt an immediate, insistent need to find expressions of *love*. I understood that I needed to focus all my attention on joy rather than on suffering, and that this was a message I needed to share.

Like many people, I had spent several years of my adult life suffering—the specifics aren't all that important. However, by the time I was knocked over by *The Gates of Hell*, I had moved from ninety percent misery to the freedom of a joyous and loving life most of the time. Self-improvement had taken conscious effort on my part and essential support from friends who were farther along the path, but I had learned to live lightly, playfully, joyfully, lovingly. My life was filled with miracles, ease, delight and wonder. Life was my Champagne River. Although I lived this life, I didn't really know how to teach anyone else how to live it.

Now I do.

What I will share with you in this book is not new. Great spiritual traditions, religious teachers, philosophers and poets have said the same things in far more eloquent ways for millennia. What I can offer you is a simple, practical handbook of seven specific behaviors that will change your life. You don't have to believe anything. Just follow the rules, use the tools and cultivate the practices, with an open mind and an open heart. Be curious, be diligent, and be willing to allow Joyful Living into your life.

On Becoming a Playful, Lighthearted, Loving Person Who Understands How Life Really Can Be Heaven on Earth

You know the difference in how you feel when you are elated, in love or wonderfully satisfied versus depressed, fatigued or overwhelmed. In the positive states of being, you feel light and powerful. Everything is easy and goes your way. Positive emotional states carry high vibration, high energy. In the negative states of being, you feel heavy, powerless and nothing goes right. Negative emotional states carry low vibration, low energy.

Most of us think that these emotional states *happen to us*. The truth is that we have more control over our emotional state than we imagine. Everything you will read in this book will help you take charge of your emotional state. You will learn how to deal with the circumstances of life—even the painful ones—and still maintain a high vibration or high-energy positive emotional state.

By following the rules and using the tools and techniques in this book actively every day, that is, by making each of these practices into a habit, *you will change who you are.* You will raise your energetic, vibrational level to the point that you will be a different kind of person. As you become lighter and more playful, more joyful, more loving, you will find life becomes an amazingly delightful experience, full of little miracles, astonishing ease and way more fun than you could imagine. You don't have to believe me. Try it yourself. What would your life be like if you were joyful most of the time?

The ideas in this book may sound crazy, but they work. The seven rules or behaviors described here are the basis of all great teachings on living a fulfilled life. They are what respected philosophers and teachers have been saying forever. They are simple truths. I'm just presenting them in another way—*with the call for you to practice them to make them habits in your life.*

Once these behaviors and tools are habits for you—and it takes only three weeks of daily practice to make something a habit—you will be astounded at the difference in your life.

INTRODUCTION

Maybe, like many people, you spend up to 80 percent of your life on automatic pilot, mindlessly making your way through each day with only an occasional reminder that you are a living, breathing human being with creative and loving energy potential.

Maybe life is scripted for you. Your days are the same, one after the other. You have the same routine when you wake up every day, the same route to work, the same conversations, same lunch, same problems, same route home, same, same, same.

Maybe whatever dreams you had as a kid have vaporized. Whatever desires you have now are ridiculed, or are kept hidden for fear of being ridiculed.

Maybe life is pretty good for you, but you worry that it will turn sour again.

Maybe you have some nagging medical problems that you are trying to ignore—or that you can't ignore any longer.

Maybe you routinely reach for a beer, a glass of wine, a martini, a joint or something else to take the edge off your life. The stress is too much. The boredom is too much. The demands are too much. The miserable relationship, environment or work is too much. Escape is the best solution you've been able to find.

Maybe there is a better way to live.

If you are reading this book, maybe you are waking up from your walking sleep, or maybe you've been awake but not very happy, or maybe you are happy but wondering how to be really, really joyful.

Whoever you are right now, welcome!

Welcome to the possibility of a life that is incredibly creative, bountiful and way more fun than you ever thought possible. Welcome to a world in which you will feel content, vibrant, or even giddy with delight. A world in which everything happens easily and just as you want it to happen. A world in which you'll laugh a lot and perhaps even inspire other people to ask how you manage to be so happy all the time. What would that be like?

Some people are afraid to be happy all the time. Some people think it's wrong or dangerous or impossible or *weird*. Some people believe that life is to be taken seriously, that there are problems to be solved and injustices to be righted. Some people don't believe they should be happy if anyone else is unhappy.

I invite you to try this thought on for a moment: If you are unhappy, sick, poor, abused or otherwise maltreated by life, will it help you become happy, well, rich or healed from life's treatment if I stand beside you projecting my own unhappiness, sickness, poverty or abuse?

I don't think so. On the other hand, if I am happy, there is the possibility that I can rouse you to happiness. If I am well, there is the possibility that I can aid you in getting well. If I am rich, there is the possibility that I can inspire you to move out of poverty. If I am healed of the abuses of life, there is the possibility that I can help you heal from those abuses.

Think what you can do for the people in your life simply by learning to live your life more joyfully!

Personal Responsibility for Your Life

One of the foundations of Joyful Living is the idea that each of us is responsible for how we feel and for how we are living our lives. If you don't fully accept that idea, consider the possibility that you *could* be in charge of how you feel and how you are living your life.

Would you *like* to be in charge of how you feel?

Would you *like* to be responsible for how you are living your life?

If you *are* intrigued or excited by the possibility of taking responsibility for how you feel and how you live your life, keep reading! The rules, tools and practices of Joyful Living will surprise you with their seemingly magical powers to transform both how you feel on a daily basis and how you live your life.

You will discover ease in making choices that benefit you and those around you. You will get to know yourself more deeply, and you'll learn to dance with whatever demons you happen to carry around with you. By the way, we all have our pesky demons. You'll learn to get along with yours until eventually they leave you because you won't be feeding them with drama, which is how they survive.

Why Are These Rules Called "Practices?"

The first three practices are very familiar rules of behavior in our society. We've all heard them a gazillion times. Pay Attention! Say Thank You! Be Quiet! As long as they are commands that we follow because we are told to by authorities external to ourselves (parents, teachers, signs in the library reading room), they remain rules of conduct imposed by society.

I invite you to begin to follow these first three rules in a different way. I invite you to Pay Attention more grandly than you are used to. I invite you to Say Thank You more profusely. I invite you to Be Quiet more deliberately. When we adopt these rules in a conscious manner—making them intentional behaviors that we practice—they have a different effect on us. They open our eyes to new possibilities and prepare us for more profound changes offered by the more advanced rules and practices.

The four advanced practices (Releasing Resistance and Fear, Heart-Centered Living, Creating Your Own Reality and Changing the World) build on the foundation of the first three. These four practices are ongoing, creative approaches to living life with intentional joy. The techniques and tools offered in each of the chapters will help you master these more complex practices.

You can "follow the rules" or "do the practices." The choice of terminology is yours. The information and instructions are the same. I'll use both terms throughout the book.

What is important to remember is that it is the conscious performance of these practices, the *practicing* of them, that allows remarkable change and growth to occur. These are not intellectual concepts that you can study and understand and be done with. Unless you use them daily, they will remain simply words and concepts, and your life won't change.

If you want to increase your aerobic capacity, you can read all about the effects of exercise and the differences that occur if you work out for twenty minutes three times a week versus an hour every day. You can find out how to measure your heart rate, what your target heart rate should be and how long you should maintain that rate. You can research the best heart rate monitors and where to buy them. You can explore various aerobic conditioning techniques, such as running or swimming or aerobic exercise classes. If you decide to choose running as your method, you can study running techniques and the best running shoes to buy. You can even find statistics on the average time in which someone of your sex and age should be able to run a mile. And you can find a runners' club to join if you happen to be a social kind of person.

While all of that is good information, none of it will affect your aerobic capacity until and unless you actually start running, and keep running on a regular basis. It's the *practice* of running that changes the aerobic capacity of your body.

Similarly, the seven rules and practices for Joyful Living will affect your capacity for joy only if you actually use them regularly. When you do them regularly, they will have a positive effect on you by bringing you greater ease and joy in your life.

These rules are also called practices because, like running or playing the piano or anything new that you begin to do, you will find yourself at first a beginner for whom the whole idea is challenging. Everything about a practice may seem strange and different. As you play with them for a while, however, the techniques become more familiar. The practices eventually become routine, habitual activities in your life.

My son Casey used to be very frustrated when his teacher gave him a new song to play on the piano, because he couldn't play it. So I put a chart on the wall, with ten boxes on it. Every time Casey played the song, he got to check one box. I encouraged him to concentrate on doing the best he could each time, and I promised him that by the time he'd checked all ten boxes, he would be able to play the song. Of course, he could play the song well by checkbox number five or six or seven, and he thoroughly enjoyed playing it with a sense of accomplishment and joy by the time he checked off box number ten.

Learning each of the practices of Joyful Living is just like Casey trying to learn a song on the piano. If you can let go of needing to be perfect the first time, and simply concentrate your efforts on practicing the practice once, twice, three times, before you know it, you will be playing the songs of a joyful life. The more you practice, the better you will play, and you will become a virtuoso of living a Joyful Life.

Before-and-after Self-Assessments

If you'd like to track your own progress along the path of Joyful Living, you are welcome to spend a few minutes on a brief self-assessment before you read any further. It is not a test; it is not required. It is available for you to use as a baseline measurement before beginning your play with Joyful Living and to use again at any point along your journey. Use it if you think it will be fun or enlightening to chart your progress. The self-assessment comes in two parts and can be found in Appendix A.

Creating Your Life as You Want It to Be

As you incorporate the practices into your daily routine, you will find that you can easily create life and all its circumstances in the way you want them to be. It sounds magical, doesn't it? Well, because we've been taught differently, yes, it appears to be magic. You are actually learning to play the game of life with a different set of rules, a set of rules that is becoming available to all of us now.[1] We do have enormous powers, and they are delightful to use.

Here are two tiny examples of what will become common realities for you as you integrate the practices into your life.

1. In our car-centered society, it seems that we are always in need of parking places. As you begin to pay attention and say thank you (the first two rules or practices), somehow

---

1. Please see Appendix B for resources concerning this topic.

parking spaces start to open up for you *right in front of wherever you want to go.* I'm not even going to try to explain it. Just follow the rules and watch this happen for you. When it does happen, remember to say thank you!

2. Sometime when you're looking for something to wear, or trying to decide what to make for dinner, or looking for the right parts and tools to complete a project, and there's *nothing* in your closet/pantry/tool shed, stop for a moment. Close your eyes, take a breath and say to yourself (out loud is even better), "I have everything I need right here, right now." Indulge yourself in really believing this statement. (This will come easily as you do the practices.) Then open your eyes and look around again. I guarantee you will find amazing and creative solutions to your attire/dinner/do-it-yourself project. And you will be *so* delighted with yourself for your creativity! (Remember to say thank you!)

A Final Note of Introduction

These practices don't *require* that you change your diet, your lifestyle, your relationships, your religion, your job or anything else. If you observe them regularly, though, you will find your perspectives changing, and those changes in perspective may shake up your life. As you integrate these new behaviors into your life, you will be training yourself to live lovingly, and that means that you and everyone you touch will be blessed, no matter the changes that seem to want to unfold in your life. You will have the choice, as you always do, to step forward, backward, sideways or off your own path at every juncture, every day, in every moment. You are free to determine how joyfully you want to live on any given day.

Let's get started by looking at the first rule, Pay Attention and the Practice of Cultivating Awareness.

If I'm not happy
in this time,
in this place,
then I'm not paying attention.

– JODI HILLS, *Studio J*

CHAPTER ONE

PAY ATTENTION

Cultivating Awareness

Those words "Pay Attention" always show up in my mind with several exclamation points and Sister Mary Somebody banging on her desk with a ruler, her angry face and raspy voice scaring us all into submission. They're not my favorite words, but they lead us to the first stage of living a joyful, loving life.

The idea is to wake up, look around you, and notice what's going on in your life right now. That's it. That's Rule Number 1. *Pay Attention.*

Paying attention most of the time requires that you increase your psychological capacity for awareness, like increasing your aerobic capacity on a physical level. Awareness requires conditioning and constant practice to maintain. Let me assure you, though, that cultivating awareness can be playful and entertaining—and you don't have to break a sweat.

Start with **Noticing Your Life Right Now**. Please do this exercise. It will take about five minutes. Remember—life is experiential, and we are beginning the process of making your life into an incredible experience. This is the very first step into that exciting, fully realized life. Reading about it is not the same as living it. Please live it!

You have some choices to help you with this exercise:

1. You can go onto our website and listen to Exercise 1 at www.dudleycourtpress.com/seven-practices.

2. You can have someone else read the directions below to you while you follow along. Read the directions slowly, pausing between each step of the exercise.

3. You can record the following directions if you have a tape recorder or voice recording software on your computer or phone and then play them back while you follow along. Read them slowly.

4. You can read the directions through once and then, keeping them nearby to glance at, you can begin the exercise.

Enjoy a few minutes of **Noticing Your Life Right Now.**

EXERCISE 1: **Noticing Your Life Right Now**

Sit comfortably wherever you are right now and close your eyes gently.

Exhale all the air from your lungs. Relax and let breath fill your lungs without any effort from you.

Exhale gently and then inhale again, paying attention to the movement of your body in response to the breath.

What happens to your body when you inhale?

Exhale, without strain, a bit more slowly this time.

Allow the breath to fill you again, deeply and easily.

Relax and let your breathing continue normally.

Listen and begin to notice the sounds around you. See if you can distinguish between sounds that are far away or outdoors if you are indoors, and sounds that are closer to you. Just notice the sounds, and then notice if you are reacting to the sounds. Let the sounds and the reactions simply be there.

Now notice what you are feeling with your physical body, first with your skin: perhaps the temperature or movement of the air around you or the texture of the fabric of your clothing.

What do *you* notice?

Can you feel the weight of your feet on the floor or the weight or pressure of other parts of your body that are supported? Your back, perhaps, against a chair? Your buttocks wherever you are sitting. Can you notice the shape of the indentation your body makes on the cushions?

Now bring your attention back to your breath. Notice the air moving in and out of your nostrils or mouth as you breathe. Can you feel the temperature of the air as it moves in and out?

Notice if you can smell anything. What odors or fragrances can you distinguish?

Breathe again, a slow, deep, relaxed inhalation. As you exhale, slowly open your eyes and adjust again to the light.

Notice how you feel right now.

How Did It Go?

Learning to pay attention to right now can be complicated if you're not used to it.

Did you notice any frustration with this exercise?

Did you notice your mind wandering away from the sensations you were trying to pay attention to?

Did you observe your mind making judgments about the noises, or smells, or about the exercise?

How interesting that in trying to use your mind to simply observe with just three of your senses (hearing, touch and smell), the mind acts like a team of runaway horses, charging into thoughts and judgments you hadn't directed it to consider.

So who's in charge here? You or your mind?

Who's in Charge Here?

The practice of paying attention, or cultivating awareness, is the practice of training the mind to focus on what *you* want it to focus on. After all, it's your mind, isn't it? How tough can it be to get it to do what you want?

Think of this practice with the mind as a dance, or a pick-up game of basketball. It's not really a competitive experience; you and your mind are just out there having fun. You need each other, and you both have some great skills. When you are paying attention, however, *you* get to decide if you want to dance or play, or if you want your mind to sit this one out.

4

The practice of paying attention, or cultivating awareness, means bringing your attention, or awareness, into the present moment over and over again. As you begin to do this, you will begin to notice how often your mind is not where you are. You will be driving to work and your mind will be on a beach in Hawai'i. Your child will be sharing details about her day at school and your mind will be at your office, preparing for tomorrow's meeting. You will be chowing down on a meatball grinder, and your mind will be on the field at the Patriot's game you are reading about in the paper. Paying attention means bringing your mind where you want it to be in this moment.

So often we live on autopilot. Unconsciously. When you are awake but unconscious, you are not really living. You are sleepwalking through life.

Waking up means breaking the cycle of autopilot living. It can be challenging at first, but with a little bit of determination, you can do it—and the benefits are huge.

Here are some ways to practice paying attention or cultivating awareness. I suggest that you pick one or two of these (not all of them) and practice them faithfully for three weeks. As they start to become habitual, you can add one or two more practices. They become entertaining games to play with yourself. Each time you practice one of the exercises, you are strengthening your ability to focus your mind. Staying in shape, in terms of paying attention, or cultivating awareness, has to be a regular practice. You don't need jogging shoes for this—just a few minutes of staying conscious every day. What could be easier?

Ways to Pay Attention:
More Tools for Cultivating Awareness

1. Use *Exercise 1: Noticing Your Life Right Now* every day—
   even twice a day—to train your brain to focus on right
   now. Don't fret that the practice will be boring. It won't be
   the same experience every time. You will discover new sensations and new levels of awareness each time you practice,
   if you really bring your attention to the exercise.

2. *Exercise 2: Stop and Ask.* Several times a day, stop whatever
   you are doing and ask yourself the following question:
   What am I doing right now? Notice your mind's response
   and then separate the simple observation of *what* you are
   doing from the judgments and feelings that your mind
   offers *about* what you are doing. Set the judgments aside
   for now and simply focus on describing *what* you are
   doing right now. You can do this for ten seconds every
   hour on the hour, every time you begin to eat something,
   every time you change locations—whatever easy signal
   works for you in your life. Try to do this at least three times
   every day at a minimum. As you practice, you will notice
   patterns of internal response. Notice the patterns. Let go
   of judgments about how well you are doing the exercise.
   Just notice.

3. *Exercise 3: Stop and Observe.* Several times a day, stop
   whatever you are doing and look around you for sixty
   seconds. Really take in what you see—things, people,
   colors, textures, movements. Pretend you are describing
   the scene to someone who is blind. Keep observing for the
   full minute, and notice the thoughts that play in your

mind after the first fifteen seconds. Keep at it for one minute. You are building awareness capacity!

4. *Exercise 4: Stop and Listen.* Several times a day, stop and listen for one minute. Listen to the sounds far away or outside, nearby or inside. Name the sounds or describe them as if you were doing so to someone who is unable to hear them. Keep up the practice for one full minute.

5. *Exercise 5: Stop and Feel.* Several times a day, pause whatever you are doing and for one minute, notice what your body is feeling. Notice the external sensations—air movement and temperature against your skin; skin against clothing; body pressure or weight against any support. Notice the internal sensations—physical discomforts, stress or pain and physical relief from gentle movement or intentional relaxing of your muscles. Maintain the focus for a full minute.

These exercises will build your awareness capacity—and the more capacity you have for mindful living, the more joy you will be able to bring into your life.

I encourage you to use these tools actively beginning today. Practice one or two of the exercises several times a day for the next three weeks. Notice any effects on you. Notice the judgments your mind makes about the exercises. Notice what your mind says about you because you are doing the exercises. Notice how you react to your mind's commentary. You might want to jot down some of your observations as you work through the exercises. You may be surprised by what you learn about yourself.

You might also like to try *The Chocolate Journey of Sensory*

Awareness, a one-hour guided audio journey into mindfulness that begins with eating chocolate. This audio was produced by HatBox Journeys, a company I cofounded. It's a delightful exploration to expand your capacity for awareness. The audio is available for immediate download at www.dudleycourtpress.com/chocolate-journey-of-sensory-awareness/.

Increasing your ability to pay attention now is the very first step on the path to a joyful life. These exercises will open your eyes. Have fun discovering the world around you and the world within.

Here's a prayer to inspire you to pay attention each day.

Sunrise

Look to this day!
For it is life, the very life of life.
In its brief course
Lie all the verities and realities of your existence.
 The bliss of growth
 The glory of action
 The splendor of achievement.
For yesterday is but a dream,
And tomorrow is only a vision.
But today well lived
 Makes every yesterday a dream of happiness
 And tomorrow a vision of hope.
Look well, therefore, to this day!
Such is the salutation to the dawn.

– Kalidasa

CHAPTER TWO

SAY THANK YOU

Expressing Gratitude

Now that you are learning to pay attention regularly to what's going on in your life, it's time to take advantage of your growing awareness to lift your spirits (and your vibration) with the second rule, Say Thank You.

Saying thank you, which is also the practice of expressing gratitude, is, hands down, the easiest, fastest way to feel better almost immediately *and* it's one of the most powerful tools for creating a more pleasing life. Even if you have to start by *acting as if* you are grateful, go ahead and pretend. It works!

How can saying thank you make your life more wonderful? When you say thank you, your brain assumes you mean that you are appreciative or grateful, and begins to send out messages to the rest of your body, which releases the good-feeling hormones known as endorphins. When you say thank you *with intention*—take just a millisecond to consciously *feel* thankful—you enhance this effect tremendously, causing an even stronger endorphin release, resulting in a stronger "feel good" response.[2]

---

2. For details on the science behind this phenomenon, see Appendix B.

To get the huge benefits of this rule, make it a game. Practice it often, abundantly and with great enthusiasm. The more you practice saying thank you, the faster you will see results and the more amazing they will be.

How and When to Say Thank You

Say thank you all the time, everywhere, over and over again, out loud, silently, joyfully, thoughtfully, looking skyward, looking someone in the eye, looking out over a landscape or parking lot or around your kitchen. Say thank you to yourself. Say thank you to your God, to the unknown mystery, to your angels, guides, or whatever you believe in.

Today, just notice how often you currently say thank you throughout your day.

Tomorrow, see if you can find more opportunities to say thank you, silently or out loud. Both methods count.

Over the next three weeks (remembering that it takes about twenty-one days of constant practice to create a habit), practice saying thank you as much as you can. Find every little and big reason you can think of to be grateful and express your gratitude openly and enthusiastically.

Say thank you when your kids arrive home safely. Say thank you when they leave to head off on an adventure. Say thank you when you finish a project ahead of schedule. Say thank you to every cashier, waitress, bus driver and toll collector. Say thank you to your colleagues at work, to your spouse, to your parents, to your room-mates. Say thank you when your cup of coffee tastes just perfect. Say thank you when you finish a great workout. Say thank you to the bird singing outside your window, to your dog when it snuggles up for a rub, to the flowers that please you with their fragrance or color. Say thank you when you find a seat on the subway, make it to the bus stop on time or catch every green light on your way to school.

Turn yourself into a geyser of gratitude and watch your own joyful energy begin to expand.

Start Your Day with a Thank You

Start every morning by saying thank you when you first wake up and realize that you're alive.

Be grateful that you have *this day* to witness, explore, discover, love, live, enjoy, and love some more.

Be grateful that you have *this day* to address whatever is wrong in your life, to correct mistakes you've made, to hug your loved ones, to finish whatever you have been meaning to finish.

Be grateful that you have *this day* to make a difference to someone.

Keep the Gratitude Going throughout the Day

When you brush your teeth, say, "Thanks for this great electric toothbrush" or "Thanks for this tasty toothpaste."

When you shower, say, "Thanks for this warm water" or "I'm grateful that I live in a home with indoor plumbing; so many people in the world do not."

When you eat your breakfast, say, "Thank you for this delicious, healthy food" or "Thanks for this easy-to-prepare food that lets me get on with the day quickly."

When you are in the middle of your commute, find something to say thank you for—the smooth-flowing traffic, the comfort of your car, a seat on the bus, the new bike route you just found, the pleasure you get from walking to work and not paying for gas.

When you are in the midst of your day, say, "Thanks for this job that provides me with income to support my family" or "Thanks for these clients who challenge me to find solutions to their problems" or "Thanks for this wonderful home that I get to live in" or "Thanks for these students whose lives I can influence."

You get my drift.

Find something to be grateful for and then find something else.

This is a simple rule with powerful effects. Gratitude is not complicated or hard or mysterious. Just express it and see what happens.

Pay Attention and Say Thank You: Play the Gratitude Game

You may have noticed that when you follow the second rule, Say Thank You, you also have to follow the first rule, Pay Attention.

The good news here is that if you can remember either one of these rules, and follow it, you can automatically follow the other rule!

If you've been practicing the first rule, Pay Attention, you can just add the gratitude part. When you stop to pay attention to what you are doing at a particular moment, notice what's going on around you, and focus on several things for which you can be grateful.

Make it a game. Set your watch alarm and play this Gratitude Game for five minutes every hour today. You may start to feel silly at first, but keep it up and notice how you begin to feel deep down in your heart. I guarantee that if you genuinely play this game for five minutes even three times a day for a week, you will find that your heart is lighter, your life seems more pleasant, you are less worried, less tense, more playful, and you will feel more alive—and happier.

Try it and see for yourself. What have you got to lose?

If you *do* practice these rules, they will soon become as natural as breathing. And, like your breath, they will provide the essential foundation for a joyful life.

When Your Day Isn't Going So Well

It's a challenge to be grateful when your kids are sick, when the dog tears up the sofa pillows, when the toilet overflows, when your boss complains about a report you wrote, when your partner forgets the one errand you asked him or her to do for you, etc., etc., etc.

What you will notice, if you are paying attention, is that there's a *constant* flow of disagreeable challenges in life for most people. The details may differ, but the flow of problems seems unending. Here's how to convert this constant flow of problems into a constant flow of invigorating joy boosters.

First, remember that all of that unpleasant stuff is just today's story. Take a deep breath and ask yourself if this problem will really matter one year, or ten years, from now. As you gain some perspective, you will know in your heart that there is something more permanent, more meaningful in your life than this particular irritation. You may not know what that something is, but when you open up to the possibility, you know it is there. Allow that awareness to blanket you, shielding you from the unlikable aspects of the present moment.

Second, look for something, *anything*, to feel grateful for in the midst of the worst circumstances. This is the magic. Focus your attention on finding something positive in the worst of circumstances and then actively *feel grateful* for it. You *will* feel better. The more attention you can pay to things to be grateful for, and the more actively you cultivate your gratitude, the better you will feel.

A hokey inspiration for expressing gratitude is that old Disney movie with Hayley Mills, *Pollyanna*. Her genuine, unwavering adherence to her father's guidance to find something to be glad about, no matter what the circumstances, inspires a whole town to open their hearts. You may want to watch the film when you are fatigued; it's a very slow-motion movie compared to modern flicks.

Do let it play over you. Get into it and feel the story. Then go out and play the Glad Game. It works.

In Moments of Crisis

Don't let any unpleasant situation get away from you before you are able to say at least one thank you in relation to it.

For example, say you are in a car accident. Rather than focusing on all the troubling details of it, find *something* to be glad about. You are only slightly injured instead of killed. Your car sustained minor damage, nothing major, or your car is totally wrecked but you wanted to get rid of it anyway.

Focus on something positive, something to be glad about, and keep your focus there! Repeat your statements of thanks over and over again. Let the rest melt away. Stay attentive to the better thoughts. *You will feel better and better.*

"This Is Stupid," Your Mind May Say

The process of growing more joyful by saying thank you becomes so playful that you may find yourself arguing (with yourself or with me) that this is all nonsense. "You can't possibly become happier by simply expressing gratitude," your mind—so used to being the old you—will argue.

The wonderful thing is that you don't have to argue back. Just notice those comments, acknowledge your mind for sharing them and then invite your mind to join you in this experiment.[3]

You can allow your mind to dismiss this idea, or you can choose to try it.

You know how you feel in your life now. If you choose not to try this, you'll never know how you *could* feel.

If you are not joyful now and want a life of joy, something will have to change.

If you experiment with this practice, something *will* change.

The Bottom Line

Practice paying attention and saying thank you every day, several times a day. Notice how you feel after several days of practice. Take the risk of gushing gratitude once a day. See what it feels like to give into it fully. You can do this without anyone knowing about it. Say your thank yous silently, especially during any geyser of gratitude moments. Remember, this is a mental game to change how you think!

---

3. As you reach this point, you are accomplishing something major. You are becoming aware that there is more to you than your body and your mind. You are noticing that you are not your thoughts. There is a part of you that is able to see what thoughts the mind is thinking, and the tricks the mind is playing. This part of you is called the Watcher or Observer.

CHAPTER THREE

Be Quiet

Embracing Stillness

My mother used to say that the real reason she went to Mass on Sundays was for the peace and quiet. As a mother of ten kids under the age of fourteen, that was the only time during the week she had to herself.

I went to yoga classes twice a week when I was a working mother of three young boys. I *know* those classes kept me sane.

Every religious tradition includes practices of embracing stillness. If we are never quiet, we lose our connection to the Divine and may even forget that it is there, waiting. Our lives become fragmented and increasingly meaningless.

Do you seek out stillness in your life?

Or does the idea of embracing stillness cause you to want to toss this book aside?

For some people, the third rule, Be Quiet, is frightening (or stupid or a waste of time). Whatever the quality of the resistance, it is often based on a fear of meeting one's deeper Self, for that is what shows up when we are quiet and still—that and/or whatever you conceive of as God.

With a little practice, you will develop a familiarity with the sweetness of stillness. When you have had that first taste of *knowing* your own deeper Self, or God, or whatever it is you find in that place of quiet, you will be drawn to this well of peace and love over and over again. When we are quiet, we are renewed. When we embrace stillness, we are infused with undeniable love.

If you are fearful, go slowly to reassure yourself that there is really nothing to fear.

Oh, for a while you may have to fight with the wild and incessant thoughts that your left brain throws in front of you as you trek towards stillness, like cutting through brambles to reach a quiet meadow. Your left brain likes to be in charge. When you choose to experience stillness for a while, it knows you're heading for right-brain dominance and it just doesn't like that. As you practice being quiet, your left brain gradually learns that you don't mean to leave it behind forever and it becomes a bit easier to manage.

Why Should You Be Quiet?

Our lives are harried, stressful, overcommitted. Our minds are busy with details, responsibilities, task lists. Levels of cortisol (a stress hormone) are too high. Blood pressure levels are too high. We suffer from sleep deprivation. When we have time to rest, we no longer know how. We escape into drugs, alcohol, the Internet, TV, etc. A good healthy nap is allowed only to old people or lazy bums.

And we grow sicker as a society.

Living a more joyful life *requires* balancing rest with action. We need to learn how to achieve a restful state so that our bodies can release tensions and toxins. We need to practice resting in order to heal and in order to reconnect with that which is deep within.

The benefits of spending a few minutes every day in stillness are detailed in Herbert Benson's classic *The Relaxation Response*.[4] Not only does a brief period of focused stillness reduce stress and evoke the body's natural healing powers, it can also open the doors to intentional creation. Please read Dr. Benson's book if you want an easy-to-understand, convincing and scientific explanation for the benefits of this practice.

Is Embracing Stillness the Same as Meditation, Relaxation or Prayer?

Sort of.

In meditation, effort is made to still the vagaries of the mind completely.

In relaxation, the intention is to let go of tension that is held both consciously and unconsciously in the physical body.

When you are actively praying or chanting, you are talking *to* God. When you stop to listen, then you are embracing stillness. There, in those moments of silent awareness when your mind is

4. Herbert Benson, *The Relaxation Response* (New York: William Morrow, 1975).

carried on the echoes of your chant or your prayer, you can hear the pulsation of response.

All of these techniques can lead to delicious moments of connection to something within us. Philosophers and others can argue whether the experience within stillness is communing with God or our unconscious self or something else. Chapter 5 of Dr. Benson's book draws on a broad array of writings from ancient to modern times and from many religious and historical sources to demonstrate the universality of these delicious moments. According to Dr. Benson, the feelings associated with the states of meditation or deep prayer have been expressed as "ecstatic, clairvoyant, beautiful, and totally relaxing . . . [at] ease with the world, peace of mind, and a sense of well-being . . . pleasurable" (p. 127).

For me, the practice of meditation or being in stillness draws me to a delightful, mysteriously almost nonphysical place where I often lose awareness of my body but experience physical sensations like tingling or buzzing, which I classify as energetic responses. I feel refreshed, relaxed, and ready to handle life with ease and grace.

What could your experience of stillness be?

How to Be Quiet,
or Embrace Stillness

You could take up Vipassana or Transcendental Mediation or you could go fishing, alone, on a quiet lake.

You could say the Rosary or repeat a mantra with your mala

beads, or you could have a cup of tea before the rest of the house-hold wakes.

You could visit a chapel, park your car at a scenic overlook or sit on a rock in a nearby woods and practice breathing consciously for several minutes.

You could sit alone in the food court at the mall or at an airport gate or on the subway, lower your eyes and take yourself inward for a few moments.

You might seek a meditation group to help you learn and grow accustomed to the practice of embracing stillness.

Often it is easier to still the left brain by tiring it with some physical activity and then consciously relaxing the body. Yoga classes are structured to give this experience.

Embracing stillness can begin with five minutes once a day, though you will derive greater pleasure and benefit if you can work up to twenty minutes once or twice a day. Perhaps you can practice for five minutes every day and add a longer session once or twice a week.

Do you feel overwhelmed at the idea of adding a new job to your life? Relax!

If you've been practicing Pay Attention and Say Thank You, you have already carved out the necessary time. Combine a couple of two-minute sessions and begin to use them to focus on stillness. Follow this simple series of steps with intention.

1. Breathe in a relaxed manner.

2. Let your mind focus on your breath instead of thoughts racing through your head.

3. Notice your body in relation to space.

4. Imagine breathing in clean, positive energy and love from the universe.

5. Imagine exhaling tension, worry and negative energy.

6. Feel gratitude in your heart for this brief moment of stillness and repeat "thank you" several times.

Consider this time a gift you are giving to yourself. As you grow to enjoy it, expand the time you give to yourself.

More Ways to Experiment with Being Quiet

During the next three weeks, choose one of these more expansive ways to experiment with being quiet:

1. Turn off the TV, radio, iPod, etc., for a day or week. Notice how much of your day is filled with the distractions of such media. Live without them for a while and notice everything you can about your reactions and feelings towards the world around you.

2. Plan a day or week without reading—no newspapers, no magazines, no mail, no books, no computer screens. Give your left brain a break from the verbal world. Spend time in nature, creating art (collages from construction paper, finger paintings—the form of expression can be quite simple). Notice how you feel before, during and after your experiment.

3. Choose a day to consciously observe conversations that come into your life—discussions or interactions in which

you participate in person or on the phone. Notice patterns, especially yours, and notice if your mind is in alignment with what you are saying, or if your mind is full of contrary chatter. Notice if your conversation comes from your heart or from some other place. How much of the conversation is useful and pleasing? How much of the conversation is wasted energy? Just notice.

If you are enjoying these experiments, go ahead and try a second one. Just don't overwhelm yourself with more "shoulds." (We'll talk about eliminating all "shoulds" in chapter 4.) Please take all of these practices lightly and joyfully. If they are working for you, you will be drawn to more. If they are done as "shoulds," you will only feel frustration and resentment, and that's not the purpose of the practices or this book. Be kind to yourself. Take it slowly. Listen to your heart.

Notice Any Resistance. Notice Any Changes.

As you experiment with embracing stillness, you will find yourself becoming more aware of how you spend your energy throughout the day. Apply rule two generously! Be grateful for the people, machinery and options that you have in your life. Be grateful that you are becoming aware that you can make choices about which of these elements you want at your life's banquet.

Play with all of the practices and techniques you have learned so far. Notice how your life is changing as you develop these practices into new life habits. Keep a journal if you can.

Are you resisting these practices?

Just notice your resistance. Give no thought to the reasons for it. Simply notice your resistance. You might say something like, "Hmmm. Isn't that interesting. I *want* to live a more joyful life, and I'm learning about some simple techniques and yet I feel resistance to trying them out. How interesting to notice this."

Don't give any energy to the process of figuring out why. You will build up the left brain resistance if you do. You can keep observing, but stay away from judging or analyzing. If you find yourself deep in explanations, stop explaining and just notice how interesting it is that you can get so deep so quickly. How amusing your mind is.

The more you can pull yourself out of the rational left-brain dominance (signaled by thought, judgment, explanation, analysis and rationalization) and simply sit in the right brain (observing without judging, experiencing without seeking understanding, being without doing), the more you are following the practices and the more joyful you will become.

For a fascinating look at how a brain scientist looks at the left brain/right brain miracle, watch Dr. Jill Bolte Taylor's riveting 2008 TED Talk. Get the link on our website: www.dudleycourtpress.com/seven-practices.

Remember that as human beings we are blessed with both right and left brain hemispheres. Over the thousands of years of human history, we have learned to harness the capacities of the left brain brilliantly. It is time for us, as humans, to recapture the brilliance of the right brain, to develop and utilize it as much as we use our left brains.

Perhaps you would enjoy using the following meditation based on Psalm 46:10. Simply sit quietly for five slow breaths, reciting one line on each exhale.

Be Still and Know That I Am God
Be Still and Know That I Am
Be Still and Know
Be Still

CHAPTER FOUR

LET IT GO

Releasing Resistance and Fear

By now you have committed yourself to staying awake in your life by paying attention. You are playing the Glad Game and saying thank you constantly throughout your day. You are taking time to be quiet on a regular basis. You feel happier a lot of the time. Serendipitous moments are becoming more frequent. Parking places and short waiting lines are showing up. Things you ask for come to you. Moments of amazing bliss are beginning to twinkle in your days.

You are on your way to Joyful Living.

The first three rules or practices (Pay Attention, Say Thank You and Be Quiet) are easy and can be done with very little effort beyond remembering to do them. They will always be part of your joyful life, as moderate exercise, fresh air and wholesome foods are a foundation for a healthy physical body. Return to these basics over and over again whenever you stray from the delicious path of Joyful Living.

Now let's move on to more challenging practices that will move you to an even deeper sense that joy is always available.

I'm Okay. It's the Rest of the World That's the Problem.

No matter how diligently you pay attention or say thank you, the world doesn't always understand your intention to live joyfully. You will find that despite your practices and your improving baseline mood, you are encountering lots of things that make you grouchy:

other people who don't do what you want them to;

institutions that want to run your life;

tasks you've undertaken that you don't want to do;

situations and crises that are no fun to deal with.

All of these disturbances interfere with your attitude of gratitude and prevent you from advancing *until you learn how to deal with them.* They won't disappear from your life; you will continue to notice these challenges and potential disturbances flowing towards you. The magic of Joyful Living is that you will begin to see these people, institutions, tasks and situations from a new perspective—a perspective that allows you to meet them with a loving heart rather than with a defensive ego.

By practicing the first three rules of Joyful Living, you are already training yourself to live from a loving heart. The next three chapters of this book are advanced training. The practices in these chapters may seem a bit more difficult because we'll be examining things most people don't ever really look at. Once you learn how to see life differently, you will find it easy and far more fun that ever before.

Optical and Other Illusions

Your experience with what we're going to explore in the next three chapters may be similar to what happens when you encounter an optical illusion. Some optical illusions provide the experience of seeing two images in one, with a foreground shifting to become the background. Other images are designed to take on three dimensions when viewed in a certain manner.

Sometimes seeing the contrasting image or the three-dimensional quality is challenging because *our belief* in the two-dimensional reality that we *know* is in front of us fights with the visual tricks employed to create the illusion. Sometimes we get a quick glimpse of the "illusion" but lose it. Eventually, however, with practice and concentration, we capture the hidden image long enough that our brain accepts its reality. Once the "illusionary" image is perceived this way, our brain *knows* it is there, so our mind doesn't have to have a struggle of belief any longer. Usually we can view the image easily and shift now at will from two dimensions to three, or from one image to the other. Whether either image is now "illusionary" is up for debate, since we can see both of them equally well.

Imagine something similar happening with your perspective on life. By following the first three rules, you begin to see and experience new ways of living, like getting those glimpses of the 3D pictures. However, these "illusionary" moments of joy and freedom run into unconscious beliefs and old patterns of thinking that insist that this much joy and freedom cannot exist.

You *know* that you are experiencing more moments of joy and freedom, and you *know* that you can shift your vision towards this new way of living. How do you break through the resistance caused by those old beliefs and thought patterns?

First, have confidence in the developing flexibility of your thinking, which you are creating by using the first three practices consistently. With that flexibility of thinking, you can intentionally take on your own resistance to these "illusionary" realities of joy and freedom. In these next three chapters, we will first examine the kinds of resistance you may be experiencing and ways to release them. Next, you will begin to identify and use your feelings to strengthen your embrace of joy and freedom. Finally, you will learn how to choose the beliefs that make the most sense for you now, graciously discarding old beliefs that no longer serve you.

These next three rules—Let It Go, Own Your Feelings and Choose Your Beliefs—are more complex and intertwined. They tend to spiral together, so don't worry if the concepts seem a bit confusing at first. You can figure out any immediate challenge by asking yourself: Is there resistance here, or am I not clear on my feelings here, or is there a belief that is causing me some discomfort here?

As you learn to play with these three advanced practices, and as you continue to use the first three tools (Pay Attention, Say Thank

You, Be Quiet), you will find yourself moving into nearly constant Joyful Living and it will be fantastic!

What Is Resistance?

Resistance, in psychological terms, is the process by which the ego keeps repressed thoughts and feelings from the conscious mind. We know that the way to Joyful Living is to expand our awareness, to own our feelings and to choose our beliefs, so dissolving resistance is part of the journey.

Resistance is not a bad thing. Often resistance is the ego/mind doing its best to keep you "safe" within the confines of your existing beliefs—so that nothing shows up in your consciousness that your ego/mind has determined would hurt you. Sometimes you need that sort of protection. Allowing the ego/mind to control your life *all the time*, however, limits your growth.

In order to live in extraordinary joy, you must live from your heart, not from your ego/mind. The first three rules are tools for opening the heart. Releasing resistance is a conscious practice of moving from the ego/mind to the heart in our experiences of life.

Fear is the source of most resistance, and fear is nothing more than resistance to love. In this chapter, we will examine some of the ways resistance shows up in our lives and learn some tools for opening to the flow of love.

For those of you who are caught in fear—and you may be hiding it from yourself under cover of aggressive achievement, shopaholism, perfectionism, anger, the need to control—be kind to yourself through this exploration. Your ego/mind has been protecting you for a long time. Love your ego/mind for how well it has tried to take care of you, even as you gently reach out with your heart to release the ego/mind's grip on your life. Love your ego/mind as you explain that it will now live within your expanding heart.

Dissolving resistance is an ongoing process. It may not take long before you begin to enjoy it, as I do. Whenever I can identify resistance, I celebrate! I know that as soon as I dissolve it, the flow of joy in my life will expand even more!

Let's look at resistance as it shows up in four key forms in our lives: Language; Irritations, Disturbances and Life Challenges; Forgiveness; and Fear of Death.

Language: "Should," "But" and "Can't"

The words we use affect and reflect how we think and feel. One way to identify places where resistance shows up in your life is to pay attention to your words as you go through your day. Notice how often you and others use the words "should," "but" and "can't." Each of these words is a red flag when it comes to your unconscious resistance.

Should. Whenever you use "should" you are invoking an external judgment regarding your behavior or thoughts. The external judgment may come from what you were told by your parents, teachers, spouse, boss, neighbor or church leaders. "Should" is not a word known to the heart, or to a life lived in joy. Can you declare yourself free of all "shoulds"?

Listen for the words "I should" in your own speech and thoughts for the next few days. Every time you hear "I should" replace it with "I want to" or "I choose to." If you can truthfully substitute "I want to" or "I choose to," then go ahead and do whatever you are contemplating, for you are doing it in freedom and joy.

On the other hand, if substituting "I want to" or "I choose to" for "I should" doesn't ring true to you, recognize that you are not acting from your heart at this time. Whatever the circumstance, you have an opportunity here to open a new door to freedom and joy. For now, just become aware of the circumstance and make a commitment to explore it further. Some of the exercises later in the chapter may help you with your examination of your more challenging "shoulds."

But. This word often stops the flow of joy when it shows up. Substitute "and" and then change the rest of the sentence with greater awareness and conscious choice. You may be surprised how often you rely on "but" as an excuse (to yourself or to others) *not* to reveal or follow your true desires. Play with this, noticing how often you catch yourself hiding from your own truth.

Notice the possibilities that open up with this example: "I'd like to make changes in my life but I don't have the time or energy right now." No discussion. Excuse is in place. Now let's replace "but" with "and." "I'd like to make changes in my life and I'm so tired and busy I don't have the energy." This new statement honors the heart's desire to make changes instead of dismissing it. Once the desire is honored, it is strengthened. The conditions preventing the desire from being realized can be explored.

Can't. Never say "can't" again. Substitute "won't," "prefer not to" or "choose not to." Again, play with this idea over several days to observe your own patterns of hiding from your own deeper truths and desires. You may be surprised!

Another shift of perspective from "I can't" comes when you use the phrase "I don't yet see the way clearly enough." This phrase allows for so much potential, instead of cutting off possibilities as "can't" so abruptly and definitely does. Try it and see how it helps shift your views of whatever you are facing.

Continuing with the example "I want to make changes in my life, and I am so tired and busy that I can't" becomes "I want to make changes in my life, and I am so tired and busy that I choose not to make them." Personal responsibility shows up right where it needs to be. Or "I want to make changes in my life, and I am so tired and busy that I don't yet see the way clearly enough." Doesn't that pique your interest in the possibilities?

Irritations, Disturbances and Life Challenges

What if all of the minor irritations, moderate disturbances and major challenges that show up in your life were things that you unconsciously invited in?

"Are you nuts?" you might respond.

"Why would I invite that obnoxious neighbor into my life?"

"No one in her right mind would invite my brother-in-law anywhere!"

"What would I want this tax problem for?"

"You think I invited this terminal illness into my life?"

None of us consciously wants any of these problems, yet we all have them. Each one of us has our own package of irritations, disturbances and life challenges. Maybe these things are in our lives for a reason, or maybe not. Who really knows?

What we do know, though, puts the truth in the old saying "What we resist persists." The disturbances in our lives are a result of our own resistance to their presence in our lives.

"Well, of course," you might say. "Who would want this crummy boss/tax bill/broken window/terminal diagnosis/cheating spouse/etc. in his or her life? Of course I'm resisting it. I don't want it! Take it away!"

So that's the situation. You don't want it in your life and it's there and you have to deal with it. Your *choice* comes in terms of *how* to deal with it. You can resist it or you can . . .

Let it go.

That's it.

Just let it go.

All of it.

Nothing that you are resisting is worth holding onto.

Ah, but that's a cop-out, you say. That person doesn't deserve to be forgiven. If I stop doing this unending task, awful things will happen. If I tell her how I really feel, she won't love me anymore. If I face the truth that someday I'm going to die, I'll lose control of my life. If I let him have his way about that, who knows what he'll want next?

So many of our beliefs stand in the way of simply letting go. We can't see the 3D picture because our minds *know* we are looking at a two-dimensional "reality." In a later chapter we will explore how to choose our beliefs. For now, let's look at how to release resistance in other ways.

Does It *Really* Matter?

My father used to have the most annoying response when I was enjoying a good griping session about how mean someone was to me, or how unfair a teacher had been or how so-and-so took more than his or her share of dessert at dinner. "In the grand scheme of things," he would ask with a loving gentleness, "does it *really* matter?"

I may not have known what the "grand scheme of things" was at the time, but somehow he always made me feel accepted and at the same time challenged to look beyond this particular moment. His question—time and time again—stopped the emotional reaction to life's "stuff" and caused me to pause—to pay attention—to the truth of the moment.

If my suffering was due to something over which I had no control, I could choose to continue to suffer or I could choose to change my attitude.

If the transgression about which I was so upset was truly serious, I could more thoughtfully examine what to do about it.

If the situation was fleeting, I could shake it off and get on with finding something more interesting to do with my time.

Although my dad's question was generally raised when I was young and the issues were not monumental (though they were to me at the time), the philosophy behind the question applies to all of us, in all aspects of our lives. His simple question—Does it *really* matter?—encouraged me to detach from what was making me miserable and to focus on what enlivened me and brought me joy. My dad's teaching was to apply love—towards myself and towards others. He was the first to teach me that love is the greatest healing salve.

My father's lessons are echoed in a passage of Robert Monroe's *Far Journeys* that describes a formula for dealing with our own resistance—to change, to circumstances, to decision points, to pretty much anything else.[5] I recommend trying this right now as an exercise for letting go of something that is holding you back from Joyful Living.

---

5. Robert A. Monroe, *Far Journeys* (Garden City, NY: Doubleday, 1985).

The A List, the B List and the C List

On a piece of paper, list everything that is standing in your way of living joyfully today. You might list people, situations, worries, physical conditions, etc. Whatever it is, put it on the list.

Go down the list and mark with an "A" anything about which you can do absolutely nothing right now. Transfer all the A items to another piece of paper. That's your "A list."

Now go down the first list and mark with a "B" anything about which you can do something right now, even if the action is simple or small. Anything on that first list about which you *can do* something goes on another piece of paper as your "B list."

So now everything you listed as an obstacle to living joyfully is either on your "A List" or on your "B List."

On another piece of paper—mark it "C list"—write down all of your dreams, desires, hopes and needs, no matter how large or small, that are not yet fulfilled.

Here comes the fun part.

Take the A list and tear it up. Toss it in the trash. As Monroe says, "Dismiss all items contained therein from your consciousness. Why waste your energy worrying about that which you cannot control?"

Take the B list and do something—anything—to move towards resolving each item on it. You may find that with some simple action on your part, you can cross off many of the B items from your list. Once you begin to tackle the other items, with just the smallest of actions, you'll find that they have less impact on how you are feeling.

Finally, pick at least one item from the C list and do something—anything—that moves you towards fulfilling that goal or dream or desire.

Do this exercise every day until you find that you no longer have an A list or a B list, and all your efforts and focus are directed towards creating the reality described by your C list.

Did the instruction to throw away the A list surprise you? It did me the first time I read Monroe's book. It took a minute of internal arguing with all that I had been taught about how to approach life and problems. My A list contained the big issues, which, despite the fact that I had no control over them, were waiting to be conquered with my hard work and clever intelligence. What a shocking idea to throw away all those critical, very important concerns!

Can you do it?

Isn't it the most liberating feeling?

Monroe's formula is an easy method for shifting your perspective and learning to live joyfully. Letting go of what you cannot control—a scary thought for many—is tremendously cathartic once you allow yourself to do it. Acting to minimize the unpleasant aspects of life is helpful and invigorating. Acting on those things that bring you joy and pleasure . . . that's how to live an outrageously joyful life!

Complaining versus Creating

Notice if you are a complainer.

Things happen in life—kids get sick, cars break down, coworkers eat all the candy, rabbits eat the flowers in the garden. Notice how much time and energy you spend complaining and talking about today's problems. If you see that you are a complainer, try this approach to move towards Joyful Living:

When you catch yourself complaining, stop. Let go of the problem or negative situation about which you are complaining and create something that brings you joy.

For example, say you ran out of gas on your way to pick up your kids at school. You were in trouble with the school *and* your kids for being late. You really didn't like the whole situation and you find yourself complaining rather than being able to shrug it off as a bad day.

Be aware that chronic complaining reveals deeper dissatisfaction, so dig a bit.

Turn your attention completely away from all that went wrong and ask yourself this: *How do I really want this part of my life to be?*

Your answer might be: *When I pick up my kids from school, I want to be on time and relaxed enough that I can enjoy them and help them let off steam or be there for whatever they need me for.*

Or it might be: *I really hate having to stop what I'm doing and run over to the school in the middle of the afternoon to pick my kids up every day. It ruins my whole day and I resent being a taxi driver. I want not to have to do this.*

Or it might be: *Sometimes I like picking up my kids, but sometimes I really would rather have the whole afternoon without the interruption.*

Notice that this process gives you a chance to tell yourself the truth about what you really want around this particular aspect of your life. If your mind takes you right away to the "shoulds," just put them to the side for a few minutes. Focus your attention on what you would *really, really, really* like around this aspect of your life, as if your fairy godmother were right here ready to wave her magic wand to make it happen just as you desire. You might even want to write some of this down so that you can play with it in pieces.

Once you have stated or written what you really, really, really want, see if there is something you hadn't noticed before. Maybe you've been so busy and stressed that you forgot that you really like spending the time with your kids after school. Maybe remembering that you really like that time with them is all you need to figure out how to change other aspects of your life to provide the opportunity to be relaxed and on time, because that is what you really, really, really want.

Or perhaps you know deep down that you *really, really, really **don't*** like the whole chauffeuring job and you can't see any way to make it more fun for yourself no matter how hard you try. Perhaps this awareness is enough to cause you to rethink how your kids get home from school. What if there were alternatives to being a chauffeur? Is there a bus they could take? Could they ride bikes? Could someone else pick them up? Could they stay after school in a day-care program? Could any of these options work even one or two days a week, so that you can create a change that makes you happier?

Notice as you play with this how often your mind will try to throw rocks at you. (*Yeah, but…*; *Are you kidding?*; *It's your job, dummy!*; *No way will that work!*)

Invite your mind to join you in imagining: *Wouldn't it be nice if I could have at least one full afternoon to myself and not have to interrupt what I'm doing to pick up the kids? Wouldn't that be nice?*[6]

You *will* find alternatives as long as you keep this process light, stay focused on what you *really, really, really* want and simply be amused at the voices of your mind that will tell you "No!" Eventually—and eventually will become shorter and shorter very quickly—this process of shifting your thinking from a state of complaining to a state of creating will become easy and playful. Remember that you will have lots of opportunities to practice. Stuff we don't like shows up all the time in life. The key to Joyful Living is simply to apply these tools to every experience and make each moment a place to generate more joy.

Example: I went to a local restaurant for lunch before an appointment at the hairdresser's next door. To make things quick I

---

6. "Wouldn't it be nice if…?" is one of the great tools for moving into Joyful Living, by the way. Anytime things just aren't going the way you want them to, stop and ask the question, following the "if" with exactly how you'd like things to be. See chapter 6 for more.

requested the special salad and asked for the dressing on the side and no cheese. Fifteen minutes later the waitress put the plate in front of me, victoriously announcing, "The cook forgot to put the dressing on the side, but she left off the cheese! Is that okay?"

My choices were to take the salad as is or go to the hairdresser's hungry. The top layer didn't look too bad, so I begrudgingly accepted the plate and began scraping dressing from chicken slices and pieces of tomato.

Under the top layer, however, the entire salad was drenched in dressing. I just couldn't eat it. I left 80 percent of the salad on the plate and went to the front to pay my bill.

"Sorry for the delay!" sing-songed the waitress as I handed over my money.

"None of it seemed to work out very well today," I grumbled, taking my change and leaving—dissatisfied with myself as much as with the lunch. I was annoyed with the service and with myself for accepting a lousy lunch. I was angry yet trying to live in joy and I couldn't figure out how to do it!

Later I realized that by not returning the salad, I took away the restaurant's opportunity to give me what I wanted. I accepted less, it made me unhappy, and I blamed them.

A week later I was at another restaurant with a friend. We both ordered salads, with dressing on the side. Life being what it is, the salads were delivered with dressing on. My friend's face fell. I didn't miss a beat. With absolute confidence—and joy—I smiled at the waitress and reminded her that we'd asked for the salads dry. I acknowledged that sometimes mix-ups like this happen and that I appreciated very much her taking the salads back to the kitchen. It was easy, pleasant, and my friend was extremely grateful. She hadn't wanted to make a fuss. I shared with her my renewed commitment to helping people provide me with what I *really, really, really* want!

The salads came back undressed and we had a lovely, upbeat lunch, unmarred by regret or disappointment in the food or in ourselves.

Ask for what you want. If you don't get it, decide if it really matters or not. If it does, then ask again in a loving way. Find a loving way to help others give you what you want. If it doesn't really matter, let it go and move on to something more fun. As long as you are coming from a loving place, a resolution will happen, one way or the other. Your clarity and love will break down resistance— either yours or theirs—so that you can move on in joy.

Forgiveness as a Way to Release Resistance

Another source of resistance to joy in our lives is the anger, hurt and resentment that we hold onto from past events. The only way to let go of those negative feelings is to forgive both the person who caused the hurt or anger and ourselves who have held it so tightly for so long. Yet we resist forgiving because we believe the other person doesn't deserve to be forgiven. Our sense of right and wrong interferes with our ability to move towards joy! Another "optical" illusion?

Let's take a look at forgiveness. When you are honest about it, who is really suffering when *you* refuse to forgive someone for a wrong that he or she has done to you or to someone else?

You are the one who is suffering!

Whomever you refuse to forgive is off having a grand time doing whatever he or she does in life. You, on the other hand, are torturing yourself, twisting in pain about whatever that person did to anger you, hurt or disappoint you, or take advantage of you.

Whatever the person's transgression, it doesn't matter!

You are the only being in this situation who is suffering, and—please take this in—until you let the transgression go, you will continue to suffer. Your suffering does not bring justice. Your suffering does not balance the scales. Your suffering—which is self-induced, especially now that you are paying attention—is your misery only. Your suffering is now your choice. Yes, that other person caused you to suffer, but you are now holding onto the pain, and only you can release it! And you can release it! That's the good news.

Once you understand and "get" the idea that you are the only one suffering when you will not or cannot forgive someone, you will understand that forgiveness is the only solution. By simply forgiving yourself for holding on so long, and by letting go of your anger, hurt or disappointment, you will free yourself—at last!—to be joyful and loving in your life.

Please note that this does not mean that, if the situation warrants, you should forgo legal remedies to right a wrong. By all means, follow through with the judicial process. However, I am talking about how you feel. If you can forgive and move on into the freedom of joy and love, you will trust the judicial system to do what it does for society.

If you are coming from a place of loving detachment, the outcome will be far superior for you than if you are coming from a place of fear, anger and desire for retribution. By releasing your anger or fear, and by focusing on strengthening your growth into joyful living, you can leave the judiciary system or other external process to deal with the transgressor, and move on in your life.

Read *Forgive for Good* by Dr. Fred Luskin if you need more encouragement, more convincing or more suggestions about adopting forgiveness as a practical method for becoming more joyful.[7]

Remember that resistance is fear, and fear is caused by a resistance to love. So opening up to love in every situation allows resistance and fear to melt away. Love is the greatest healing salve.

Fear of Death as a Reason for Resistance

Let's finish our examination of resistance with the big one that many people don't like to talk about.

Death.

For many people, death is a frightening concept. The thing is, we all know that someday we are going to die, as is every person we

---

7. Fred Luskin, *Forgive for Good* (New York: HarperCollins Publishers, 2002).

know and love. At least, the physical self is going to cease to function. Personally I find it comforting to believe that there is something eternal about my being that will continue to exist in some form or another after this particular physical body I currently inhabit is used up. My belief about this may be different from yours, and that's just fine. It doesn't really matter what you or I believe about life after death. Remember that our beliefs are just that—beliefs. They are not necessarily truth. No one really knows what death is all about, but each of us can choose to believe what we wish to believe about it. So choose the belief that serves you now.

What we *do* know is that the passing of this physical self is most likely going to happen someday.

We also know that the date and time of death are not generally something we can know for sure.

So there we are—we're all going to die, but we don't know when, or how, for that matter. And we don't know what "death" really means.

That's a pretty big concept, don't you think? We arrive here on this planet, maybe get to do all that treacherous growing up, pay our bills or not, maybe take a cruise and then poof! We're gone.

We could spend our time contemplating the uselessness of it all. Or we could steep ourselves in fear of the unknown. Or we could decide to make the best of it. We're here, after all. Why not decide to have a great time, reaching for as much joy as we can?

Releasing any fear of death is an important step towards living a joyful life. Fear of death underlies many other fears in our lives.

Since we know we're going to die anyway, and we know that our loved ones are going to die anyway, if we can get comfortable with those ideas, we can let go of many other fears that plague us.

Find a time when you can be alone and quiet for thirty minutes or longer. Have a journal or pad of paper and a pen or pencil handy. Invite yourself to explore your attitude towards death—your own death as well as the deaths of those you love—as a practice in releasing resistance on your way to Joyful Living.

Exercise A:
To Release the Fear of Death

To begin to release the fear of your own death, take paper and pen in hand and ask yourself these questions:

1. Are you ready to die tomorrow? If not, why not?
   List all of your reasons.
   Take your time.
   Go deep.
   Stay present.

2. What if you knew you were going to die six months from now and you had complete freedom to live your life however you wanted to during those six months? How would you spend the next 180 days?
   Take the time to be truthful with yourself.
   Trust your own wisdom.

What would you really want to honor in yourself?
What really, really, really speaks to you?

3. How different is your answer to Question 2 from how you are actually spending your life now?

    Stop here and rest for a while. Be still.
    Let your deeper knowing sort this out for you.
    Let the wisps of joy lead you to greater understanding.
    Look for inspirations that lead you towards your heart's truest desires.

4. If you were scheduled to die six months from now, are you satisfied with all of your personal relationships?

    What would it take for you to be able to answer "yes" to this question—for every relationship that is important to you?

5. If you were scheduled to die six months from now, are your financial arrangements in place?

    What would it take for you to be able to answer "yes" to this question?

6. Are your personal belongings reasonably well organized?

    What would it take for you to be able to answer "yes" to this question?

7. Is there anything you particularly want to do before you go?

    What would it take to make your answer to this question a reality?

When you finish answering all of these questions, take some time to look over what you have written. If you'd like, apply Monroe's formula by categorizing your responses as A list (things you have no control over), B list or C list items. Then you can toss the A list, take an action on every B list item, and spend most of your time focusing on your C list.

Meeting the reality of death by being prepared—mentally, financially, domestically and in terms of relationships with loved ones—allows greater relaxation and joy in every day of living. Knowing how your present life compares with the life you would live if you knew you would die soon gives you the opportunity to make changes that really mean something to you. Making these changes is part of Joyful Living because doing so allows you to move closer to living the life that you really want to live.

Exercise B:
To Release the Fear of a Loved One's Death

Have paper and pen handy. Sit quietly for a few minutes, paying attention to your body as you breathe gently.

Bring to mind your loved one—a parent, spouse or partner, child, friend.

Imagine a large bubble in front of you. Fill the bubble with pictures, thoughts, memories, images of your loved one. Take some time to recall many beautiful moments, days of total delight with this person. Perhaps add images that reflect your wishes for the future, plans you may have together or dreams you know he or she hopes to make real.

Set the bubble aside now, knowing it will be there anytime you want to return to it.

Now take paper and pen in hand and answer the following questions.

1. If you knew that your loved one was going to die six months from now and there was no way to change this, what do you imagine would be the greatest challenges for you during the next six months and after your loved one died? *Take your time here. Be gentle with yourself. Be honest with yourself. Imagine the worst and write it down. List everything that would be hard for you.*

2. For each item you wrote in response to Question 1, see if you can identify it as emotional or logistical. For example, worry about loneliness is an emotional issue. Concern over managing finances or house maintenance is a logistical issue. Not wanting to feel grief or the pain of loss are emotional issues.

3. Now mark each item you have listed with one or more of the following designations: A—I am afraid of this feeling or experience; B—I don't know what to do about this challenge; C—I don't want these feelings or experiences.

Put the list aside for a while and bring the bubble back into your mind. Sit with the loving images you have placed in the bubble. Let them surround you. Feel gratitude for the relationship you have with this loved one. Fill your heart with joy. Focus your attention for a moment on any feelings of regret or incompleteness that you might notice, and write down those observations. Are any issues or questions arising in your mind's dialogue with your loved one? Write them down. Ask yourself how you can make this bubble of images and feelings about this loved one completely full of joy and contentment. Write down any ideas or thoughts that come to you.

When you feel complete, allow the bubble of images to move aside again and bring your attention back to your paper.

You have probably discovered some areas in your relationship with this person that deserve some loving attention. Note if they are logistical or emotional. Write down the problem and see if you can offer yourself a solution as well.

If this is very difficult for you, talk with a counselor or friend. This exercise is meant to move you through the fear of a loved one's death so that you can more authentically experience life with that person now and life alone after he or she has gone. By clearing away the panic and the jumble of emotions that most of us face when we begin to contemplate the loss of a loved one, we allow ourselves to deal more clearly with the logistical issues that are usually resolvable once we accept their inevitability. We also open the way to clear decisions on how we really want our relationship with that love one to be *now*. We *cannot* change the fact that death will come. We *can* bring joy to the life we share now so that our bubble of memories and thoughts expands infinitely with love.

Getting past the fear of death opens the door to living life with an open, joyous heart.

Let It Go—Recap

1. The first step is, as always, to pay attention. Notice the resistance. Take a deep breath and release.

2. Change your language—"I should" becomes "I want to" or "I choose to." "I can't" becomes "I choose not to" or "I don't yet see the way clearly enough."

3. Look at whatever you are resisting and ask: *What would it be like if I just allowed it to be there without resisting its existence?*

4. Ask, *"Does it really matter?"* If it does, deal with it with a loving heart.

5. Let it go.

6. Apply Monroe's formula—the A list, the B list and the C list. Remember to throw away the A list!

7. Shift from complaining to creating.

8. Ask this: *I wonder if (what you really, really, really want) could happen?* Notice if you are throwing rocks at yourself. Stop throwing rocks at yourself.

9. Ask this: *Wouldn't it be nice if (state what you really, really, really want)?*

10. Forgive.

You might use the prayer on the following page as a way of releasing resistance. It is the prayer many Reiki practitioners are taught in the tradition of Reiki master Dr. Mikao Usui.

Just for today

Just for today, I let go of anger.

Just for today, I let go of worry.

Just for today, I give thanks for my blessings.

Just for today, I do my work with integrity.

Just for today, I am kind to every living creature.

CHAPTER FIVE

Own Your Feelings

Heart-Centered Living

I moved from urban California at the invitation of a friend to be a caretaker on a small cattle ranch in southeastern Arizona. I knew the difference between a cow and a horse and was pretty sure I could tell a mature bull from a baby calf, and that was about the extent of my livestock vocabulary. My career as a caretaker was short-lived. However, my years in rural Arizona have yielded a somewhat more sophisticated ability to distinguish among the quarter horses, Arabians, paints, mares, fillies, geldings, stallions and the bulls, longhorns, javelina, deer and antelope that play around here. Nevertheless, I still marvel at the conversations among some of my horse-loving or cattle-ranching friends who throw around terms like withers, Brahmins, geldings and bays. I wonder if I will ever learn to make the distinctions they do regarding these animals. I don't always see the differences and I definitely don't yet have the vocabulary to express them.

I console myself with the knowledge that any new territory

brings with it the challenges of new vocabulary. The ability to discriminate among details of your environment is essential to survival—knowing a rattlesnake from a king snake is not trivial in the desert. Mastery of any field begins with learning the jargon, the vocabulary.

Which, in a rather random way, brings us to *feelings* . . .

Naming and owning your feelings—your emotional responses to the happenings of the world around you—is the next level of practice to becoming a master of Joyful Living. Feelings are the vocabulary of the heart. As we become more tuned to the heart's messages, we are more able to live a heart-centered life.

For many of us, the first challenge is allowing ourselves to acknowledge the *existence* of our feelings. The next task is to name them. The final part of the practice is learning to own your feelings, to take responsibility for them.

Acknowledging Feelings

Many of us have been taught to keep our feelings under wraps. For some, this training occurred early, when we were very young children or perhaps in school. Others have learned in relationships later in life that our true feelings are best kept hidden away.

How and when we learned to suppress our feelings isn't all that important. In fact, focusing on the how and when and why keeps us tangled in the negative drama and story, which definitely inhibits Joyful Living.

If acknowledging your feelings is a challenging practice for you right now, that's okay. You can apply the rules, tools and practices of Joyful Living that you have learned so far to help. Start by exploring, in the following exercise, any subject, issue, relationship or problem that presents itself in your life right now and seems to be holding you back.

Exercise: How Do I Feel About _____?

1. Take a sheet of paper and write across the top of the page the following question:

   How do I feel about _____? You fill in the blank. It could be "my job," "my spouse," "my kitchen," "how I behaved at the party last night" —anything you want to explore.

2. Exhale fully. Take a deep breath, then exhale with an audible sigh, shaking off any tension you might be holding.

3. Draw your attention to the present moment. Notice how you are sitting, and where. Notice the sounds around you. Notice any smells. Without reacting, notice what is going on around you. Pay attention to your present moment.

4. Find something in this present moment to appreciate. Perhaps it is something you see, or something you hear. Perhaps you can feel grateful for simply having this moment of time to be. Practice saying thank you for a couple of minutes, really feeling the gratitude in your heart. Say thank you for the opportunity to grow and learn.

5. Now you will simply ask for understanding of how you feel about the subject you are contemplating. Read the question

that is written at the top of your paper. Sit quietly for a moment as the sensations begin to flow. You may wish to write words or draw pictures on your paper as responses come to you. Simply record what comes. There is no need to analyze or respond to it now. Just write or draw it on the paper. If sensations come without words or pictures, try relating the sensations to the four simple designations of mad, sad, bad or glad to help yourself begin to distinguish them.

6. Notice if you sense any resistance to your deeper knowing. Your mind may fight with the feelings, especially by trying to draw your attention to the story or drama around the subject. Invite the mind to set the story aside for a while and join you in listening to what the deeper, feeling self has to express.

7. Once you have one or more feelings listed—even if it is just one of the mad, sad, bad, glad words—set the paper aside. At this point, the goal is simply to identify and name the feelings you are experiencing relative to the subject you chose to explore.

8. Now notice your reaction to the exercise. Notice if you found it scary or helpful. Notice if it was easy or difficult to name your feelings about the subject you were practicing with.

If you found the above exercise scary or threatening, and you completed it anyway—congratulations! It takes courage to explore territory that frightens us.

If you found the exercise helpful, wonderful! You are learning how to cut through the jungle of the mind to find the true, heart-centered guideposts—feelings—for Joyful Living.

You can use this basic exercise to explore any issue in your life, large or small, and to identify the feelings you have around the issue. We'll get into the next step—deciding if that feeling is one you wish to continue to feel, or if you want to find a better feeling—later. In the meantime, here's an example of how this process of acknowledging and identifying feelings occurred for me.

Allowing Feelings to Surface

During my journey towards Joyful Living, I spent several years in the emotional numbness of a challenging relationship—when allowing or expressing my true feelings just didn't feel safe. We all adapt for self-protection and survival, and my adaptive, constant feeling state was "okay." I was rarely angry, disappointed or frightened. Nor was I often excited, enthused or joyful. I existed, deferred and sought refuge in yoga and writing, believing that eventually the day would come when I would be released from my emotional prison.

When I finally extricated myself from that unhappy marriage, I found myself almost illiterate when it came to distinguishing my feelings. I could tell if I was mad, glad or sad—sort of like I could tell a horse from a cow from a bull—but the finer distinctions among emotional states were lost on me.

I also knew that without knowing more about how I felt, I couldn't really know how to fix what wasn't working in my life, so I took advantage of an opportunity to attend a workshop with Marshall Rosenberg on Nonviolent Communication. (See www.cnvc.org for more information about Marshall Rosenberg's extraordinary work.)

By the time of the workshop, I was beginning to live pretty joyfully much of the time and serendipity was a constant companion. Some of my buoyancy was a reaction to having been stifled for so long, and I was also actively seeking opportunities for emotional and spiritual growth. My focus at the time was learning about myself in relationship with men, as I had managed to lose my Self in that recently ended twenty-five-year marriage.

A very attractive man, on whom I had a wild, unreciprocated crush, was also at the Marshall Rosenberg conference. I flirted a bit, as I did whenever our paths crossed, as they did from time to time. We were walking together towards the snack bar during one of the breaks. I was feeling happily certain that our mutual appearance in this place was once again proof that we were destined to be together. (We all have our dramas, remember?) I anticipated a heartfelt, profound conversation with a caring, supportive friend.

"So how's your business going?" he asked with obvious interest in my well-being.

"We finished the first CD and it's off to the manufacturer right now!" I responded, proud of our tangible accomplishment.

Shaking his head from side to side, he knifed through my enthusiasm with a focus on something entirely different. "You've got to get your marketing plan in place. That's the most critical thing," he said.

I felt confused, disappointed, thrown off base. Our conversation continued for a few more minutes, but I wasn't really paying attention anymore. I was distracted and didn't quite know why. I drifted away from him as we approached the snack bar and avoided him for the rest of the day.

Later that night—around two in the morning—I was suddenly awakened from my sleep by—who knows by what. I don't want to say I heard voices, because I didn't. Not exactly. Not out loud. It was more like a strong sense of knowing, something that I've experienced many times before. It always seems to be a small group "speaking" to me and I can translate the "knowing" that I experienced from THEM like this:

THEM: "OK, dear one. It's time to work. Up and at 'em." (I call THEM my guides; my guides have quite a sense of humor.)

I sat up in my bed, ready for instructions.'

THEM: "Play back that conversation with Mike."

So I did. When we got to the point where he said, "You've got to get your marketing plan in place. That's the most critical thing," THEY said, "Stop. What are you feeling in this moment?"

I started to answer. "Well, at this moment in the conversation, I feel . . . ah, well . . . um . . . ah. . . . I don't know exactly."

THEM: "Well, stick with it. Stay right in this moment. Feel it. What is going on for you right then and there?"

I spent *two hours* sitting up in my bed trying to answer that question.

No kidding. Was I angry? No, not really angry. How could I be angry with Mike? I was madly in love with him. Was I sad? Sort of, but why should I be sad when I was talking with the guy I had a wild crush on? Was I happy? No, I know I wasn't happy, and that made me sad because I was talking with the guy I had a wild crush on. Was I insulted? No, and that would have been terrible because I was talking with the guy . . .

Every time I tried to give up, They would firmly and lovingly insist that I continue to sit with the recollection until I could express how I felt in that particular moment.

It was a great challenge, in part because I didn't want to acknowledge that the guy on whom I had such a wild crush didn't give a hoot about how I was feeling, and if he didn't care, then . . . well, I didn't want to go there. Oh, how we play such games with ourselves!

Finally, after almost two hours of inner dialogue, I went back to the scenario one more time. I played it again, with commentary.

"So how's your business going?" he asked with obvious interest in my well-being. *See, I know he's interested in me. He's really concerned about me and my business. He's my friend, and we'll probably start dating any time now. I'm feeling great! In love!*

"We finished the first CD and it's off to the manufacturer right now!" I responded, proud of our tangible accomplishment. *I know he'll be impressed by this. We've spent two years getting to this point, and I'm so pleased that we're doing so well on the production end. I'm celebrating! He's going to be so pleased for me!*

"You've got to get your marketing plan in place. That's the most critical thing," he said, bluntly. *Huh?... Ouch!... Ah, what about the CD?...Ahhh...oh dear.*

What was dramatic for me was how hard it was to get to the point where I could actually say—and this came out in a very, very small voice at first—that I felt bad and sad. I didn't want to allow for that possibility, because I was convinced that Mike and I were destined to be great lovers and he would never make me feel bad or sad.

My own denial was the first thing I had to break through.

Once I allowed myself to *feel* what I was really feeling, and to say it out loud (even in that tiny voice), it became much easier to accept, and to allow the actual feeling simply to be there. Then I could look at it and use the knowledge I'd gained at the conference to recognize that I felt sad and bad because my need to be acknowledged hadn't been met. All I had wanted from Mike in that moment was a smidgen of recognition, validation, credit. And because I didn't get that, I dropped out of the conversation with him and felt crummy.

We experience negative feelings when a need we have is not being met. We experience positive feelings when our needs *are* being met. That's Marshall Rosenberg's message.

When I let go of the story I had manufactured around the two of us, I was able to explore the reason for my negative feeling—the need that was not met—which was that I was not acknowledged in my moment of triumph.

I couldn't express my feelings easily because I wasn't familiar with what feelings felt like and I wasn't comfortable allowing myself to have needs! I'd suppressed negative feelings for so long that I didn't know what to do with them. It wasn't easy for me to understand that I was feeling *disconnected* from him because I didn't get the acknowledgment I needed, that I was *disappointed* in our interaction.

An Inventory of Feelings and Needs

The following Inventory of Feelings and Needs was produced by the Center for Nonviolent Communication (www.cnvc.org) and reflects the work of Marshall Rosenberg. Make copies of it and put one by the phone, on the coffee table, by your computer—wherever you might be when you are engaged in conversation with someone (verbal or written)—and use the list of words to help you identify how you feel.

Then play some of the games that follow, to develop your fluency with the vocabulary of feelings and to understand what feelings you are familiar with and what feelings you would like to feel most of the time. You do not have to be a victim of emotional reaction. Believe it or not, you can learn to use the feelings you have to guide yourself into nonstop Joyful Living!

When you need to, use these tools to learn why you are experiencing negative feelings by identifying the need you have that is not being met. Address the issue if it is significant to the health of a meaningful relationship.

POSITIVE FEELINGS – *The Glad List*[8]

ENGAGED	REFRESHED	AFFECTIONATE	JOYFUL
Absorbed	Enlivened	Compassionate	Amused
Alert	Rejuvenated	Friendly	Delighted
Curious	Renewed	Loving	Glad
Engrossed	Rested	Open-hearted	Happy
Enchanted	Restored	Sympathetic	Jubilant
Entranced	Revived	Tender	Pleased
Fascinated		Warm	Tickled
Interested	**PEACEFUL**		
Intrigued	Calm	**GRATEFUL**	**EXHILARATED**
Involved	Clear-headed	Appreciative	
Spellbound	Comfortable	Moved	Blissful
Stimulated	Centered	Thankful	Ecstatic
	Content	Touched	Elated
EXCITED	Equanimous		Enthralled
Amazed	Fulfilled	**HOPEFUL**	Exuberant
Animated	Mellow	Encouraged	Radiant
Ardent	Quiet	Expectant	Rapturous
Aroused	Relaxed	Optimistic	Thrilled
Astonished	Relieved		
Dazzled	Satisfied	**CONFIDENT**	**INSPIRED**
Eager	Serene	Empowered	
Energetic	Still	Open	Amazed
Enthusiastic	Tranquil	Proud	Awed
Giddy	Trusting	Safe	Wonderful
Invigorated		Secure	
Lively			
Passionate			
Surprised			
Vibrant			

---

8. These charts are based on Marshall Rosenberg's Inventory of Feelings and Needs. Copyright 2005 by Center for Nonviolent Communication. Website: www.cnvc.org. Email: cnvc@cnvc.org. Phone: +1-505-244-4041.

Negative Feelings – The Bad, Sad, Mad List

VULNERABLE	AFRAID	EMBARRASSED	ANGRY	AGITATED
Fragile	Apprehensive	Ashamed	Enraged	Alarmed
Guarded	Dreading	Chagrined	Furious	Disturbed
Helpless	Foreboding	Flustered	Irate	Rattled
Insecure	Frightened	Guilty	Outraged	Restless
Leery	Mistrustful	Mortified	Upset	Shocked
Reserved	Panicked	Self-conscious	Disgusted	Startled
Sensitive	Petrified		Hateful	Surprised
Shaky	Scared	TENSE	Horrified	Troubled
	Suspicious	Anxious	Hostile	Uncomfortable
AVERSION	Terrified	Cranky		Uneasy
Animosity	Wary	Distressed	FATIGUED	Upset
Appalled	Worried	Distraught	Beat	Irritated
Contemptuous		Edgy	Burnt out	Aggravated
Disgusted	SAD	Fidgety	Exhausted	
Dislike	Depressed	Irritable	Lethargic	CONFUSED
Hateful	Dejected	Jittery	Sleepy	Ambivalent
Horrified	Despairing	Nervous	Tired	Baffled
Hostile	Despondent	Overwhelmed	Weary	Bewildered
Repulsed	Disappointed	Restless	Worn out	Dazed
	Discouraged	Stressed Out		Hesitant
ANNOYED	Disheartened		DISCONNECTED	Lost
Aggravated	Forlorn	PAIN	Alienated	Mystified
Dismayed	Gloomy	Agony	Aloof	Perplexed
Disgruntled	Heavy-hearted	Anguished	Apathetic	Puzzled
Displeased	Hopeless	Devastated	Bored	Torn
Exasperated	Melancholic	Grief-stricken	Cold	
Frustrated	Unhappy	Heartbroken	Detached	
Impatient	Wretched	Hurt	Distant	YEARNING
Irritated		Lonely	Distracted	Envious
Irked		Miserable	Indifferent	Jealous
		Regretful	Numb	Longing
		Remorseful	Removed	Nostalgic
		Repulsed	Uninterested	Pining
			Withdrawn	Wistful

NEEDS

CONNECTION
Acceptance
Affection
Appreciation
Belonging
Cooperation
Communication
Closeness
Community
Companionship
Compassion
Consideration
Consistency
Empathy
Inclusion
Intimacy
Love
Mutuality
Nurturing
Respect
Safety
Security
Self-respect
Stability
Support
To be known
To be seen
To be understood
Trust
Understanding
Warmth

HONESTY
Authenticity
Integrity
Presence

AUTONOMY
Choice
Freedom
Independence
Space
Spontaneity
Learning
Mourning
Participation
Purpose
Self-expression
Stimulation
To matter
Understanding

PEACE
Beauty
Communion
Ease
Equality
Fairness
Harmony
Inspiration
Order

PHYSICAL WELL-BEING
Air
Food
Movement/exercise
Rest/sleep
Sexual expression
Safety
Shelter
Touch
Water

MEANING
Awareness
Celebration of Life
Challenge
Clarity
Competence
Consciousness
Contribution
Creativity
Discovery
Efficacy
Effectiveness
Growth
Hope

PLAY
Joy
Humor
Jocularity

Words of Caution

Do *not* use this tool in a power-trip sort of way. "I feel angry because my need for you to do the dishes wasn't met so you better do them now." Uh-uh. That's not how this works. You may have a need, but it is *never* someone else's responsibility to meet your needs. The other person can *voluntarily* choose to act in such a way that your need is met; he or she can never be commanded to meet your needs. You can state your feelings and describe the need that wasn't met. The other person has every right to say, "Tough cookies." And that's that. You still have a choice about how you want to feel. However, you cannot demand that anyone else be, do, think or act in any particular way. The other guy gets to choose his way of living joyfully too.

Learn more about this at www.cnvc.org if you are interested.

To stay focused on Joyful Living, I encourage you to improve your facility with the vocabulary of *positive* feelings. The more you practice positive feelings, the more you will live in positive feelings.

Regardless of what is going on in your life, what is important is to acknowledge how you feel *now*, and to take responsibility for that feeling. First you must recognize that you are feeling *something*. Then you get to decide, consciously, whether or not you like the particular feeling, and if not, to find a better feeling. A rather radical concept, don't you think?

So how do you begin to decide whether or not you like a particular feeling and to choose a different one? Once you get past the idea that it's radical to choose how you feel, you'll need some practice with the possibilities and choices. Here are some games to get you started.

Game to Play with Feelings

This game will help you learn how specific feelings actually feel to you. This is particularly helpful if you've spent many years shutting down your feeling Self, or denying yourself any feelings. Remember that this is a game you are playing for yourself. There are no rights and wrongs. It's not a test. It's just a chance for you to sample a smorgasbord of feelings in a safe way.

What Does _____ Feel Like to Me?

Point to a word on the Feelings Vocabulary list. You can pick out the word intentionally, or you can just let your finger drop to the page and use the word your finger lands on. I encourage you to focus on the positive feelings.

Consciously pretend that you are feeling that feeling. Use your imagination. What does it actually *feel* like to you? Can you capture a distinct image or physical sensation of how that particular feeling feels to you?

If you have a hard time getting a clear sense of the feeling, can you imagine what someone else might feel in his or her gut or heart if he or she were feeling that particular feeling? Have you seen someone in a movie experiencing that feeling? What did it feel like for that person? Sometimes pretending we are someone else helps free the emotional body to experience something that would be too challenging for our mind to accept for ourselves. Pretending helps us open up when our mind or social conditioning is too much in charge.

If you are really stuck in No Feeling Land, try contrasting strongly positive and strongly negative feelings. The wide differences will be easier to experience. What happens to you when you are extremely angry? What happens to you when you are very happy? What happens to you when you are terribly sad? What happens to you when you are really scared?

Practice imagining the sensation of several feelings several times every week for several weeks. Notice your increasing fluency and confidence in naming your feelings.

The following exercise will help you gain a sense of your "normal" emotional state and help you change it if you wish.

What Are My Baseline Feelings and Are They Consistent with Joyful Living?

Review the lists of feelings and check off the ones that are familiar to you.

Notice if you are more familiar with negative feelings or positive feelings. (Be assured that as you practice Joyful Living, you will be feeling positive feelings most of the time!)

For each of the feelings you checked as familiar, ask yourself how often you have felt that feeling in the past week or month. If you like a particular feeling, see if you are feeling it often enough to suit yourself. If not, make a commitment to feel that particular feeling more often.

Notice if any feelings seem foreign to you as you go down the list. For every feeling that seems strange or unfamiliar, ask yourself if you would *like* to feel that feeling sometime. If you would, mark it with a different mark.

Decide to explore the underrepresented and unfamiliar feelings in any way you choose. You might add one per day to your "to do" list and then consciously find a situation in which to feel today's feeling. You might play a game with yourself, asking, "What would it feel like to me to feel this feeling?"

It is quite reasonable and possible to decide on any given morning that today you will feel, say, *amazed* as often as possible during the day. Then you have a little game to play with yourself—looking for opportunities to genuinely be *amazed*. As you go about your daily life, you can keep asking yourself: *What is amazing about this? If this were not my regular, habitual route to work/coffee shop/copy machine/coworker/etc., what might I find amazing about it/him/her?* This may sound like a bizarre way to spend your time, and yet, when you try it, you just may find that it's a lot more fun than listening to talk radio or gossiping at the water cooler. I can guarantee you that if you play this game with a genuine spirit of exploration, you will discover all kinds of astonishing perspectives, ideas, delights and joys.

As you identify feelings that feel good, keep them! Decide to feel them more often. Practice feeling them more often. Focus on creating more of the positive. Let the negative feelings fade.

Know that as you continue to practice the rules of Pay Attention, Say Thank You, Be Quiet, and Let It Go, you will become more attuned to your feelings. With the help of these exercises, you'll find that you are more often feeling positive feelings rather than negative feelings. With the help of your growing vocabulary of feelings, you will be able to say "*This* is how I feel!" quickly and confidently.

Remember, if you don't like how you feel, you can look to your list of feelings to find something that would feel better. We will work more on consciously changing the beliefs that often underlie feelings in the next chapter. For now the critically important step is getting to the point of knowing how you feel and owning up to it.

Own Your Feelings—Recap

1. Learn the vocabulary of feelings.

2. Explore what all those feelings feel like.

3. Pick the feelings that feel best to you and decide to live in them as much as you can.

4. When you are not present in your chosen feelings, pay attention! Ask yourself what is going on that is causing you to move into feelings you prefer not to feel. Say thank you to the feeling itself for causing you to look more closely at your life in this moment. Be quiet and ask for clarity if you need it.

5. Ask yourself if the source of your bad feeling is something you are resisting, or if it is a condition "out there" that

causes a programmed response in you. Can you let it go? Do you have to feel the way you do about it? Can you choose a different feeling, something that feels better?

6. Look at the list of feelings and see if you can find one that feels a little better—still authentic to you right now, and a tiny bit more positive.

7. Consider how you would *like* to feel and ask yourself what it would take to move yourself closer to that feeling. Don't think in terms of what other people would have to do, or what circumstances would have to change, because you have no control over those things. You have control only over how you feel, so that's what needs to change.

Learning livestock jargon is no different from learning the vocabulary of feelings. Learning to be fluent in the language of feelings is critical for being able to identify and own them. And owning your feelings is essential to living a joyful life.

As so many teachers tell us, our feelings are our internal guidance. The better we feel, the more attuned we are to the whole purpose of life. Joyful Living is our birthright—and sometimes we have to dust ourselves off a bit in order to experience this level of bright, joyful, heart-centered living. Owning our feelings is a method for dusting ourselves off.

Owning your feelings *will become easier the more you do it.* As you tune in to your feelings, and continue to express gratitude and let go of resistance, you will begin to feel free enough in your life to express your genuine state of being. That sense of freedom will invite you to live from your heart—the source of Joyful Living.

Believe nothing, no matter where you read it,
or who said it, no matter if I have said it,
unless it agrees with your own reason and
your own common sense.

– THE BUDDHA

CHAPTER SIX

CHOOSE YOUR BELIEFS

Creating Your Own Reality

All of us hold a multitude of beliefs—about ourselves, other people, animals and plants, how the world works, the past, present and future, authority, duty, love, etc. A belief is a conviction or acceptance by the mind of the truth or reality of something "based upon grounds insufficient to afford positive knowledge," according to the American College Dictionary. That is, a belief is a statement or doctrine that a person has accepted or chosen to affirm as true. Beliefs are not objective absolutes. They reflect choices made from among alternative possibilities.

Of course, many of our beliefs are statements or doctrines that have been in our minds for so long that we don't question them. Often we don't know they are there! The ideas may have been put into our heads by our parents, our local culture, teachers, peers, our church leaders, the media, the scientific community or the government. Unconscious beliefs are statements or thoughts that circumscribe our reality without our knowledge. As we grow into greater awareness of who we are and how we feel, we gain the ability to change the boundaries of our reality, first by becoming aware of unconscious beliefs, and then by examining them. We can choose to continue to hold a belief, or to replace it with a belief that is more appropriate for us now.

This chapter will show you how to do that.

Caution

For many people, questioning beliefs can be threatening, disorienting, or downright unthinkable—at least at first. If you are one of these people, take this chapter slowly. Notice if you are gripped by fear, anger, distrust or defensiveness as you read these words regarding your ability to choose your beliefs. Just notice the feeling. Acknowledge it and wonder if there is something to be learned here.

If you can, invite yourself to continue to explore the jungle of beliefs that controls your thinking. Remind yourself that there are no lions or tigers here to jump out at you. This is an exploration of the tangled vines of thought in the mind.

We are going to explore—with paper and pencil, not a machete—ways to find a pathway that is peaceful and joyous. You can always turn around or pause if the mental effort feels too challenging. You can always come back to this place tomorrow when you feel refreshed and perhaps curious again. The choice to move forward, go back, or stop for a while is always yours.

As Abraham says, "a belief is just a thought that you keep thinking over and over again."[9] Once you understand this, you can make your own decision about whether you want to keep thinking that same thought "over and over again."

Meeting Unconscious Beliefs

As you have been exploring the exercises in this book, have you bumped up against some of your beliefs? Perhaps as you wrestled with resistance, you came up against a belief concerning your duty to your parents or spouse or children. Perhaps as you reached for joy, you were stymied by a belief about money or sex. Perhaps as you examined your feelings, you met beliefs about what is allowed and what is not.

Releasing resistance and learning to live from the heart by owning your feelings are both practices that invite us to examine our beliefs on a regular basis.

Back in chapters four and five, I suggested some tools that began to touch our field of beliefs. "Act as if . . . ," "Wouldn't it be nice if . . . ," "I wonder if . . . ," and "What if . . . " are openings to new possibilities that gently flow our thinking around unconscious and conscious beliefs that often block our path to joy. Here are some examples of how to use these tools.

---

9. See www.abraham-hicks.com for books, CDs and workshops.

"Act as If . . ."

Whenever you don't believe yourself to be quite up to a task or challenge, imagine who would be. You might envision someone you know, a mythological figure or even a character like Superman. Imagine that person taking on your challenge as you. That is, act as if he or she is working through you to accomplish the task.

For example, I don't consider myself particularly artistic (a belief I stubbornly choose to hold). I count myself blessed to have many friends who are talented artists and designers. Sometimes I am called upon to create something lovely—a table setting or a gift basket, for example. Instead of listening to the litany of negative thoughts that used to flood my head ("I can't do this. I don't know how to make this room look pretty. I always mess up these things"), now I act as if I were one of my artistic friends. "How would Amelia tackle this?" I wonder. Suddenly I am able to see the room or the gift basket with her eyes, and a joyful confidence wells up. It's as if Amelia is creating the beauty using my hands. When it is done, we both stand back and admire the always satisfying result. (Someday I'm going to sit with sketchbook in hand and wonder, "How would Monet draw those lilies?")

You can use this tool to meet physical as well as mental challenges. The only trick is to truly get into playing the part. Pretend you are Michael Phelps and you will swim faster.

Another example: Years ago I was an assistant vice president at a large bank. I wanted very much to be promoted to vice president. As assistant vice president, I believed myself to be inconsequential, unnoticed by higher management, and lacking the stature, authority and independence I wanted. I grumbled for a while, waiting for a promotion. Then I tried out "Act as if." I didn't use a stand-in here. I just went to work *acting as if I were* a vice president. I held myself to the standards I believed a vice president should have. I concerned myself more with the company's goals and objectives. I confidently greeted the executive managers when opportunities arose. I initiated projects and improved the quality of my work products to vice-presidential level. Within two months, I was promoted.

"Act as if" works when you genuinely get into the act in order to affect your own feelings and accomplishments. It has nothing to do with manipulating anyone else or pretending on a superficial level. It's a tool to change who you are so that you become who you want to be.

"Wouldn't It Be Nice If . . . ?"

This question, "Wouldn't it be nice if . . . ?" and its cousins, "I wonder if . . . ?" and plain old "What if . . . ?" cleverly draw back the belief curtains to offer us entirely new scenes to consider. They are key creative tools to use as you examine the beliefs that hold you in unhappy, unproductive or unsatisfying places.

Again, these questions can be used for physical as well as mental circumstances. My partner occasionally suffers severe leg cramps. For a long time, he would catch the initial twinge that signaled a cramp was about to begin and he would quickly move into a defensive pose to fight the painful pull on his muscle. He believed, from his past experience, that the pain would become excruciating if he didn't brace himself.

One time, after learning about the "Wouldn't it be nice if . . . ?" technique, he used it when that little twinge started. "Wouldn't it be nice if my leg relaxed completely and there was no cramp?" he asked himself. A minute or two later, when no cramping had occurred, he told me what had happened. He has successfully warded off those painful leg cramps on several other occasions since then, each time simply drawing his attention to another possibility and allowing it to become his reality.

I use "Wouldn't it be nice if . . . ?" any time circumstances are not pleasing to me. "Wouldn't it be nice if those loud people next door would quiet down so I can sleep?" They do. "Wouldn't it be nice if this boring meeting would end soon?" It does. "Wouldn't it be nice if I had more time with my girlfriends?" Phone calls and unplanned visits occur.

Does it always work so perfectly? No. Sometimes I have to wait a bit, or sometimes I change my request to make it easier for my preferred reality to manifest. "Wouldn't it be nice if this traffic jam broke up quickly so I can get to my meeting on time?" might become "Okay, then wouldn't it be nice if all of these drivers stayed calm, including me, and that even if we're stuck here for a while, our days will flow smoothly?" When I eventually arrive, my tardiness is not an issue; something else has delayed the proceedings.

There are tricks to using these questions, of course.

You have to mean what you are saying. You have to allow yourself to relish the potential you are expressing, and yet remain unattached to the outcome. You have to learn to savor the latent reality you have created. The more you enjoy the possibility, the more likely the outcome will reflect that possibility.

Convenient Beliefs

Many of us routinely create convenient beliefs to avoid facing situations we believe will be untenable. Do convenient beliefs block the flow of joy in your life?

Several years ago, I was terribly distressed in my marriage and saw no escape route. Believe it or not (and I am embarrassed to admit this, but it is absolutely true), I had convinced myself that I needed a million dollars before I could divorce my husband, in order to continue living in the expensive city we lived in and to maintain the very middle-class life we lived there with our three sons. For months I bemoaned my fate, sentenced to misery with no way out.

A new and very wise friend sat with me one evening as I complained about my horrid situation and the impossibility of leaving the marriage anytime in the next ten years. Gently, she suggested that I consider some "What ifs . . ."

"What if you were given $500,000 tomorrow? Could you proceed with a separation and divorce next week?"

Immediately, I let go of the need for a million! Five hundred thousand in hand would certainly do it. I would figure out a way to make it work. I started to feel better immediately. I could see freedom as a distinct reality now. *My entrenched beliefs shifted in an instant.*

Then she asked me, "What if you were given $250,000? Would that be enough?"

Well, it wasn't as good as $500,000, but, well, yes. I could see making it with a quarter of a million.

In one short conversation, the desperation and hopelessness of my situation shifted to possibility. Oh, there was no way I would end up with $250,000 or anything close to that, but the process of exploring "What if?" alternatives rapidly opened my eyes to the way I had constructed my reality by believing I couldn't leave my marriage without a million bucks in my hand.

Once my eyes were opened, I kept them open. I continued to explore with "What ifs" and the Belief Game, which I will explain a bit later in the chapter, until I discovered that the belief I held about the money I needed was actually an expedient, impossible condition I'd set because I was afraid to move towards divorce! As long as I couldn't get my hands on a million dollars, I didn't have to face the challenges of going through with a divorce. Once that convenient belief was challenged and exposed, I had to look at the true feelings I had about ending my marriage.

Are you hiding behind convenient beliefs in your life?

Are you convinced that you can't leave a boring job, a disastrous relationship, an unhealthy living environment?

Ask yourself "What if" questions that reflect a change of status not of your doing:

What if I were fired from this job?

What if this person who makes me so miserable decided to leave me?

What if I were invited to move from here?

Notice your deepest, heart-centered responses to these possibilities. If you feel a sense of relief or gratitude at the prospect of change, know that this is your path.

If you refuse to consider the possibilities inherent in these change-of-status questions, please see the next section, "Resistance to 'What Ifs.'"

Keep exploring this mesh of beliefs by asking questions like:

Wouldn't it be nice if I worked in a job I enjoyed and where I felt valued?

Wouldn't it be nice if we agreed that this relationship is not good for either one of us?

Wouldn't it be nice if I lived where I could walk to work and have a small garden?

Move towards your heart-centered desires this way. Write down all the answers you have to these questions. Keep asking more "What ifs?" and "Wouldn't it be nice ifs?" See what ideas and possibilities begin to emerge as you explore.

What happens if you *act as if* you were changing your job, relationship or home?

Like releasing resistance, facing our convenient beliefs can be scary. However, as soon as you begin to explore those places of tension and dissatisfaction in your life, you are beginning to open the flow of joy. Nothing has changed in the world except that you have spoken a new possibility. Yet it is this speaking of new possibilities that begets the creative solutions to all of life's challenges.

Resistance to "What Ifs"

If you are unhappy about something and you resist even the simplest "What if . . . " investigation directed towards opening possibilities for you, you might ask yourself why. Why is it so important that you hold so tightly to a belief that causes you to suffer?

Allow your answer to spill out, perhaps in your journal. If you have been following the practices for Joyful Living regularly, you are likely to find gold here in this pocket of resistance. Strands of self-protective justification always lead to a fear. If you can reach the fear and name it, you can find the beliefs, or thoughts, that are creating the fear.

Remember that this is all still in the jungle of the mind. Untangling the thought patterns that underlie the beliefs that create the fear is not always easy. However, when you identify the beliefs and then the thoughts . . . ah-ha! Now you can examine them. When you examine them, you can choose to keep them or to let them go, replacing them with thoughts and beliefs that sustain you now.

Here are some questions to help you break down your resistance to thoughts, beliefs or reasons standing in the way of your joy.

What am I resisting and what do I believe about this subject?

In order for this reason, statement or belief to be true, what else do I have to believe?

For each statement or belief, ask this:

In this moment, do I believe this statement because I know it to be true based on my own experience, or do I believe this statement because I have been told it is true?

There's nothing wrong with believing something you have been told yet have no personal experience with or knowledge about. Being aware of the *source* of your belief may be important. How did this particular belief get into your head in the first place? Is the source of the belief one that you now decide is valid?

Don't get too caught up in where the belief came from. The more important question to ask is this:

Do I choose now, in this moment, to believe that this statement is true?

Untangling Your Beliefs: The Belief Game

If you find that some of your thoughts and beliefs are just too scrambled for the "Act as if" and "What if?" approaches, you might want to try the Belief Game. It is a powerful exercise that cuts through the assumptions, learned responses and unconscious thinking that cause us to be stuck in old, limiting thought patterns.

How to Play the Belief Game

Take a sheet of plain paper and, leaving an inch or two at the top, draw a line down the middle of the page. In the blank space at the top of the page, write a word or two about the topic you are going to examine. It could be "my relationship with men," "money," "sex," "my job," "the problem neighbor next door," "my body," "my car" . . . anything, really, that is standing in the way of your feeling joyful right now.

Down the left side of the page, write as many sentences about this topic as you can, starting each sentence with the words "I believe that . . . " Your sentences will be things like:

I believe that my car is old and worn out.

I believe that I need a new car.

I believe that I deserve a new car.

I believe that I don't have the money for a new car.

I believe that if I get a new car, my sister will be jealous.

I believe that if my sister is jealous, it'll serve her right for being such a jerk.

Just keep writing sentences beginning with the words "I believe that . . . " and continue until you have exhausted all possible beliefs associated with this topic at this time. Don't be shy about filling the page. Keep mining for those deep beliefs, no matter how incidental the issue seems. Try to write at least twelve to fifteen statements, more if you can. Let yourself go—no one needs to know what you're writing on that paper. You are clearing out some cobwebs and clutter from the belief closet of your mind. Keep going until you have brought out every single belief about this topic and placed it out here in the daylight on the page.

Now, go back to the top of the list of beliefs and, on the right side of the page, write *an opposing statement beginning with the words "I believe that . . ."* Don't just write the same sentence with the word "not" inserted. Write a statement that is 180 degrees opposite of the sentence on the left side of the page, whether it is true or not. Remember, this is a game!

So, continuing with the above example, I might write the following statements about my car:

I believe that my car is new and functional.

I believe that I need an old, beat-up car.

I believe that I deserve an old beat-up car.

I believe that I have the money for a new car.

I believe that if I get a new car, my sister will be pleased for me.

I believe that if my sister is jealous, it will be sad and maybe just a momentary thing.

The next step—this is where the fun begins—is to *notice your reaction* to each of the pairs of sentences. Especially notice the belief statements that set off a strong reaction within you, positive or negative.

The belief statements that cause a strong reaction are the beliefs that you *really* want to examine, because they have a strong hold on you, and thus on your thoughts, and thus on the reality you are creating for yourself.

Play with the pairs of beliefs. Some of them are no-brainers; others will surprise you by creating resistance in you or by opening your eyes to new possibilities.

For example, when I look at my list of beliefs about my car, I have no problem sticking with my belief that my 1994 Volvo is old and worn out. No one could possibly think otherwise.

The second and third pairs of statements—*I believe I need/deserve a new car* vs. *I believe I need/deserve an old, beat-up car*—offer me a continuum to consider, rather than an either-or. The defensiveness underlying the belief statements that "I need/deserve a new car" is gentled when I give myself permission to consider the opposite statements. Once I choose not to accept the belief that I need or deserve an old, beat-up car, I feel freer to explore all the other possibilities, including the possibility of a slightly used car.

When I consider the statements about how my sister will feel, I *know* that the belief I wrote in the first column is really what I truly believe is *true*. When I read the 180-degree opposite statement, that if I get a new car, my sister will be pleased for me, I get a little kick in the stomach—could that statement *possibly* be true? And what does my emotional charge around this pair of statements tell me?

Which statement would I *prefer* to believe?

Once you get into some of the meaty stuff here, keep at it. Try to write out other, related statements around the highly charged or more interesting beliefs. When you find these triggers, these hot buttons, it's like finding buried treasure! Take the time to sit with the awareness of how each of these key beliefs is shaping your reality.

The really fun part of the Belief Game is that you get to choose which belief suits you best from each pair—or you can continue crafting belief statements until you find the ones that meet your deepest needs or match your deepest truths right now.

Continuing with the above example, the truth is that I would *prefer* to believe that my sister will be pleased for me. If I move from believing that she will be jealous to believing that she *might* be pleased for me, I release a whole truckload of negative energy and open the door to possibilities of greater joy. However, I just don't buy it. So maybe I will write the statement: "I believe that if I get a new car, I would like my sister to be pleased for me." That statement is true for me. Now I can get into it a bit more.

I can explore my relationship with my sister a bit. I can write out what I believe about her and what I believe she thinks or believes about me. It can get very interesting. Eventually, I might get to statements like: "I believe that if I get a new car, my sister will be pleased or jealous or something in between and that I have no control over how she feels." "I believe that if I get a new car, it would be nice if she were happy for me." "I believe that if I get a new car, I can keep it low key rather than try to make her jealous, which I often do." "I believe that I really would prefer a better relationship with my sister overall." "I believe that I could do much better at being a loving sister."

You get the idea.

Every time I do this exercise, I am astonished at how angry and defensive I can get about a simple statement I've written on a piece of paper. However, I also know when I hit on one of these highly charged statements that I have just struck gold! I am angry and excited at the same time, because I know that I have just found the secret to my resistance. All I have to do is keep wrestling with my beliefs or thoughts until I see them clearly. When I hold them next to alternative beliefs about the same or related subjects, then I can freely choose the beliefs upon which I will build my world.

The final step in playing the Belief Game is to rewrite the beliefs you have chosen around the topic you've been exploring. For example, I might end up with a list of beliefs that looks like this:

I believe that my car is old and worn out.

I believe that I need a newer car.

I believe that I deserve a newer car.

I believe that I have the money for a newer car.

I believe that if I get a new car, I would like my sister to be pleased for me.

I believe that if I don't try to make her jealous, she might be pleased for me.

I believe that I really love my sister and I don't have any control over her reactions.

I believe that my sister really loves me.

I believe that getting a newer car is my own choice.

I believe that nurturing a better relationship with my sister is also my choice.

I believe I can do both in harmony.

Keep this list with you for the next few hours, days or weeks, depending on the subject and your skill at keeping the vines untangled. Read the list of beliefs you have chosen frequently, to remind yourself. If, after a while, some of the statements do not ring true, play the game again to smooth the disheveled thoughts.

Once you become proficient at the Belief Game, you will find yourself whipping through most of the mundane issues that come up. You'll notice that these stumbling blocks to Joyful Living—which used to be so dramatic and important—become like knots in shoelaces. They just take a bit of attention and patience to untangle. Every time you play the Belief Game, you'll find yourself developing a greater awareness of who you are and what makes you happy.

Choose Your Beliefs—Recap

There is great power in choosing your own beliefs. Untangling thoughts that impede joy and examining them in the light of day is an adventure into increased awareness, understanding and true creative force.

Anytime you are not totally joyous, and you want to be, consider first if you are paying attention and expressing gratitude. Set aside time to be quiet and explore the impediments to joy. Any resistance to Joyful Living serves as a signpost regarding your beliefs. You resist what you believe is not true, even if that belief is unconscious. So dig into your beliefs:

1. Take the thoughts out of your mind and put them on paper. Preface every justification, excuse and reason for remaining unhappy about something with the words "I believe that . . ."

2. Then take each statement and ask yourself if you really, truly believe that statement, or if there is another statement that is closer to truth for you.

3. Use the "What if . . . ?" and "Wouldn't it be nice if . . . ?" questions.

4. Try the "Act as if . . ." approach.

5. Consider the "Resistance to 'What Ifs?,'" if appropriate.

6. Play the Belief Game.

Once you begin to realize that you can choose which beliefs you will hold, you are free to create your own reality.

Remember that the belief statements you end up with must be truthful for you now. You can use statements like: "I believe that it would be nice if . . ."; "I believe I would like . . ."; "I believe that it could be possible that . . ." Statements like these open your mind and heart to possibilities without insisting that you claim a truth that is still a bit of a stretch.

As you explore your beliefs about a subject, perhaps over time you may find yourself able to move from exploratory, tentative statements into statements that are more definitive. In either case, you are shaping the reality in which you are living your life. As you learn to explore and choose your beliefs, you become more and more the master of your life. You don't have to be subject to whims and emotions or outside circumstances. You choose your feelings and the thoughts and beliefs from which those feelings spring.

"We must develop our inner beings to become love. We may beautify this world as much as we want, but without love, it is like decorating a corpse. To beautify this world, we must carry out experiments in love. Only love can bring unity and remove the separation among all living beings."

– SWAMI KRIPALU,
a contemporary yoga master

"Approach love and cooking
with reckless abandon."

– THE DALAI LAMA

CHAPTER SEVEN

LIVE LOVE

Changing the World

If you have been practicing the tools and techniques of Joyful Living, that is, if you are paying attention, expressing gratitude and taking time to reflect, and if you are untangling the webs of fear, negative feelings and inhibiting beliefs that keep you from living a life of utter joy, then you have all the tools you need to enjoy Joyful Living for the rest of your life.

This last practice, Changing the World, is the independent study portion of this course in Joyful Living. It's the part you create as you go along, and you do it out in the world.

This is the chapter you will write.

You know enough to make conscious choices all day long about how you feel and how to make yourself feel more joyful when you want to. You know how to meet any fear or resistance that shows up. You know how to reorder your beliefs so that they don't impede your inner journey into self-realization and joy.

As you engage with the outer world, you can bring love, compassion, possibilities and inspiration to the people and situations around you at home and at work. This is the time to take all you've learned on the road. It's time to live love, carry out experiments in love, and change the world.

Conducting experiments in love to change the world is a delicious practice that the world desperately needs from you. All it requires is conscious effort to shift your thinking and to act intentionally with love. You've been doing this with your own thoughts internally. This final practice calls on you to use your knowledge to bring joy and creative responses to life's circumstances involving others.

Living love is not just about being nice or thoughtful or kind or generous in the normal course of events. Experiments in love are conscious actions to turn your own heart around when you are angry, hurt, frustrated, irritated, etc. Experiments in love don't require anyone else's participation. You are not trying to change anyone else. You will change the world by bringing in more love. Others will change as they are surrounded by more love.

I'm including just a few ideas and examples of how to live love. I invite you to begin experiments in love today. Approach them with "reckless abandon."

Beaming Love

This is one of my favorite, secret practices. When I am in a frustrating situation like coping with a recalcitrant child, dealing with an obstinate bureaucrat or even waiting in a security line at the airport,

I often reach a point when authority, rationality or patience is not enough to clear the path. Frustration remains, and increases if I keep pushing against the situation. If I am lucky, I remember the practice of Beaming Love.

I take a breath and shut off the flow of authority, rationality or patience. I switch gears, consciously moving my attention to my heart, and intentionally opening to the flow of love. I imagine the left side of my brain powering down as the right side powers up. I ask for love to flow from my heart towards the person or persons around me. I say to myself, "I really love this child and that's all there is. Everything else will work itself out," or "I send love to this clerk, who has his or her own challenges in life and can probably use an extra dose of love." In the airport security line, I send feelings of love to each person in line, and to the TSA employees who spend their days checking our shoes and bottles of liquids.

Invariably, as I concentrate on generating a flow of love, something changes in the circumstance. The child and I both feel the relaxation of tension, and suddenly we hug one another. The clerk and I feel the relaxation of tension, one of us finds something kind to say and the transaction becomes easier. The wait in airport security becomes a meditation, and a bath of loving energy for me.

This technique requires a bit of courage, because you may feel silly at first. Of course, no one needs to know what you're doing. You may be surprised at the reaction you get. Your "target" won't know what happened, but he or she will feel the effects of your loving energy, guaranteed.

An Experiment in Love: The Donation Request

To fund its budget, our rural fire department depended on donations, especially from the annual Auction Dinner. I requested a donation for the auction from an affluent community member whose home, including furnishings and artwork, was up for sale. I had assisted her on some complicated business issues for which I was not compensated, so I expected that she would make a donation out of consideration for what I had done for her.

When she flatly turned me down, I was flabbergasted. Whatever warmth I felt towards her vanished. I was hurt, and infuriated by her lack of generosity. I just couldn't believe she could be so stingy.

I suffered with this anger all day and overnight (as did anyone who came in contact with me). Around ten o'clock the next morning, however, I had a stern talk with myself. I pointed out that she was still a human being, deserving of love, and that her lack of generosity was her issue. It didn't have to be mine. I didn't have to carry around any feelings about it at all. I could get on with my day and leave her behind. Gratefully, I did. I lightened up, allowed the joyful feelings to flow again and moved forward.

Not an hour later, I received an email from this woman. She apologized for her "Scrooge-like" response to my request and told me that she was writing a check to the fire department and would mail it that afternoon.

Coincidence? Or perhaps something more mysterious. Could my experiment with loving and accepting her have released something in her heart? Beaming Love has strong effects.

Other Experiments to Try

Many early readers of this book have suggested specific areas where the challenges of living joyfully all the time are particularly acute. Four areas of great challenge are living joyfully with children, as caregiver, with a partner and in the workplace.

For living joyfully with children, experiment with love instead of control.

As a caregiver, experiment with love rather than duty.

In a relationship, experiment with love versus expectations.

To live joyfully in the workplace, focus on clarity, integrity and creativity and experiment with love rather than defensiveness.

Reorganize Life to Make Time for Living Love

As you have explored your fears, feelings and beliefs, you have probably identified some changes you want to make in how you are living your life. Living joyfully means taking action to implement those changes.

You may need to reorganize some parts of your life to allow love and joy to bloom. Perhaps you have recognized that you want a stronger relationship with your son or daughter. You may have to intentionally reserve time to devote to the practice of having a loving relationship, just as you would reserve time for tennis practice.

Osho, another spiritual teacher of this age, suggested using the term "relating-ship" instead of "relationship" in order to force our attention on the active nature of a bond between people. I like the term, and use it to keep my awareness level high in my connections with those I love.

If your "relating-ships" are important to you and yet are unsatisfying, carve out time to explore them, invigorate them, re-create them. You don't have to know exactly what to do in the time you set aside; you can just be in the relating-ship for that time and see what playfulness might unfold.

Brag about Yourself: Let Your Light Shine

Bragging about yourself when you live love, or do anything else that brings joy and light to the world, is not socially acceptable behavior in our society. It's okay to complain and share negative thoughts and actions, but tell someone that, while you waited in the airport security line, you consciously filled your heart with love and mentally sent it out, wishing your fellow travelers an easy and safe trip—no, you would be considered very, very weird if you told anyone you did this.

Nor does this make for captivating social chitchat. And what a shame.

What would life be like if we encouraged one another to share amazing stories of living love? Wouldn't it be nice to share our experiments in living love with one another?

I say, celebrate your successful experiments in love—recognizing that an experiment is successful even if it "fails"—as long as you learn something from it. Be adventurous. Be outrageous. Be courageous.

Lead with your heart to bring love into situations where it may have been absent. How much love can you bring into your work environment? How much love can you offer to cultural or racial groups to which you do not belong? How much love can you bring home today?

A Final Note

Living love, and living a joyful life, takes work, at first, and sometimes during particular episodes in your life. Sometimes being grumpy or angry is easier. The thing is, you now know it is always a choice. Share your knowledge with your friends and family and coworkers. Invite them into the magic and delight of Joyful Living.

Now we come to the end, which, of course, is the beginning. From here, the joy is in living love, experimenting with love, every day. All the techniques and practices you have learned are in your tool bag, ready to be brought out to meet the ever-changing challenges of life, to aid you in choosing and creating joy all the time.

As a friend is fond of saying, "How much joy can you stand?"

The choice, as always, is yours.

APPENDIX A

Self-Assessments

Part A

How satisfied are you right now in these areas of your life?

	Not at all satisfied							Exceptionally Satisfied		
Physical	1	2	3	4	5	6	7	8	9	10
Mental/Emotional	1	2	3	4	5	6	7	8	9	10
Spiritual	1	2	3	4	5	6	7	8	9	10
Relationships	1	2	3	4	5	6	7	8	9	10
Work	1	2	3	4	5	6	7	8	9	10
Financial	1	2	3	4	5	6	7	8	9	10
Living Environment	1	2	3	4	5	6	7	8	9	10

APPENDIX A

Self-Assessments

Part B

What's the maximum level of happiness you think is possible for you in each area?

	Not much				An Average Amount					Off the charts!	
Physical	1	2	3	4	5	6	7	8	9	10	++
Mental/Emotional	1	2	3	4	5	6	7	8	9	10	++
Spiritual	1	2	3	4	5	6	7	8	9	10	++
Relationships	1	2	3	4	5	6	7	8	9	10	++
Work	1	2	3	4	5	6	7	8	9	10	++
Financial	1	2	3	4	5	6	7	8	9	10	++
Living Environment	1	2	3	4	5	6	7	8	9	10	++

APPENDIX B

Resources

1. Hundreds of books have been written about the phenomenon of the awakening consciousness. My favorite authors and teachers include: Wayne Dyer, Marianne Williamson, Deepak Chopra and Abraham, through Esther Hicks. Read their books, listen to their CDs, and learn. Other resources that have helped me immeasurably include Neale Donald Walsch's *Conversations with God,* Julia Cameron's *The Artist's Way* and Arjuna Ardagh's *The Translucent Revolution.* Ellen Solart's book *The Art of Heartaculture* is a delightful guide to letting your feelings be your guide. *A Course in Miracles* was foundational.

2. Regarding mind/body science, Deepak Chopra, M.D., Candace Pert, Ph.D., Bruce Lipton, Ph.D., Dharma Singh Khalsa, M.D., and Dan Siegel, M.D., among many others, have penned eminently readable works relating to the biochemical and neurological foundations of mind/body connections. As Siegel puts it in an overview of his 2007 book *The Mindful Brain*: "the mind (the flow of energy and information we direct by the focus of our attention) can change both the activity and then the structure of the brain." There's plenty of science out there if you are interested.

BIBLIOGRAPHY

The following is a partial bibliography of some of the books that have influenced and guided my journey. The authors and teachers noted in the Resources section, whether listed here or not, have been exceptionally influential.

Ardagh, Arjuna. *The Translucent Revolution.* Novato, CA: New World Library, 2005.

Benson, Herbert. *The Relaxation Response.* New York: William Morrow, 1975.

Cameron, Julia. *The Artist's Way.* New York: Jeremy P. Tarcher/Putnam, 1992.

Hawkins, David R. *Power vs. Force.* Carlsbad, CA: Hay House, 2002.

Hicks, Esther, and Jerry Hicks (The Teachings of Abraham). *Ask and It Is Given.* Carlsbad, CA: Hay House, 2004.

Khalsa, Dharma Singh. *Meditation as Medicine.* New York: Simon & Schuster, 2001.

Lipton, Bruce H. *The Biology of Belief.* Santa Rosa, CA: Mountain of Love/Elite Books, 2005.

Luskin, Fred. *Forgive for Good.* New York: HarperCollins Publishers, 2002.

Monroe, Robert A. *Far Journeys.* Garden City, NY: Doubleday, 1985.

Myss, Caroline. *Anatomy of the Spirit.* New York: Three Rivers Press, 1996.

Osho. *Love, Freedom, Aloneness.* New York: St. Martin's Griffin, 2001.

Page, Susan. *If We're So in Love, Why Aren't We Happy?* New York: Harmony Books, 2002.

Redfield, James. *The Celestine Prophecy.* New York: Warner Books, 1993.

Shah, Idries. *The Sufis.* Garden City, NY: Doubleday, 1964.

Solart, Ellen. *The Art of Heartaculture.* AuthorHouse, 2005.

Steiner, Rudolf. *Knowledge of the Higher Worlds and Its Attainment.* New York: Anthroposophic Press, 1947.

Tolle, Eckhart. *The Power of Now.* Rev. ed. Novato, CA: New World Library; Vancouver, BC: Namaste Publishing, 2004.

Walsch, Neale Donald. *Conversations with God.* New York: G.P. Putnam's Sons, 1996.

Whitman, Walt. *Leaves of Grass.* New York: Viking Press, 1959.